The dark side of a great city

Evil London

Peter Aykroyd

WOLFE PUBLISHING LIMITED
10 EARLHAM STREET
LONDON WC2H 9LP

CONTENTS

© 1973 Peter Aykroyd
© 1973 Wolfe Publishing Limited
SBN 7234 0480 1

Printed in Great Britain by
Morrison and Gibb Limited
London and Edinburgh

Hogarth's 'Gin Lane', engraved by Adlard and published in 1749, where the environment created its own evils.
RADIO TIMES HULTON PICTURE LIBRARY

CHAPTER ONE

EVIL AND THE ENVIRONMENT

Here malice, rapine, accident conspire,
And now a rabble rages, now a fire;
Their ambush here relentless ruffians lay,
And here the fell attorney prowls for prey;
Here falling houses thunder on your head,
And here a female atheist talks you dead.

London! the needy villain's gen'ral home,
The common sewer of Paris and of Rome;
With eager thirst, by folly or by fate,
Sucks in the dregs of each corrupted state.

WHEN SAMUEL JOHNSON wrote these lines, the severity of both crime and punishment in London was approaching a peak. Lord North, the Prime Minister, was robbed by a highwayman in Gunnersbury Lane in 1784. Ninety-seven people were executed for assorted offences in 1785 in London and Middlesex alone. In 1801, a 13-year-old boy was hanged for stealing a spoon. By 1819, there were over 220 offences punishable by death and as late as 1833 a boy of 9 was sentenced to death at the Old Bailey. His crime was that he inserted a stick through a broken shop window and took two pennyworth of printer's colour.

If this period in time was a nadir in London's history, there were plenty of events before and in the century after which demonstrated that most Londoners went through life with a horrific background of plague, fire, grinding poverty, riot, slaughter, persecution, murder, perversion, robbery, rape and vice.

It can be argued forcefully that the lives of many modern Londoners are still tinged with many of the same appalling crimes and misfortunes; that London is not unique in evil compared with, say, Paris and Rome mentioned in Johnson's poem; and that certain unfavourable developments are always constant in urban growth. On the other hand, it can also be shown that London's trade during the eighteenth century increased some five times. However much London's character and image is assessed in this connection, it is clear that London's depraved reputation was shaped by environmental, economic and social factors in a manner entirely individual. While it is the purpose of this book to show a large collection of historical weeds, a look at the garden in which the weeds grew would help to show why they flourished.

There were three constant factors in the formation of London's evil character. The first was the urban overcrowding, linked closely with poverty, squalor and crime. This can be seen in real terms in every major city of the world. The second was the tendency of people in rural areas, faced with crises such as famine or unemployment, to move in large numbers into the cities. The third constant, again illustrated by many modern industrial cities, was urban decay, a process which evolves over a long period. In a small industrial community, masters and workers live and work side by side. However, as the village or

1541:— In this yere was burned in Smithfield, a child named Richard Mekins, this child passed not the age of XV. yeres, and somewhat as he had heard some other folkes talke, chaunced to speake against the Sacrament of the aultar. This boye was accused to Edmond Boner Bishop of London, who so diligently folowed the accusacion, that he first found the meanes to Indite hym, and then arreigned hym, & after burned him.

Edward Hall, *Chronicles*.

town grows, land values increase, and factories, artisans and the poor have to move to new, crowded settlements ringing the original community. The next stage is when with continuing prosperity, the masters and merchants move out of the town or city to live in outlying suburbs. One major result is that the city centre becomes a residentless area devoted to commerce while the poor tend to be isolated in teeming pockets of urban 'jungle'. This simplification can be carried on through further developments and improvements such as rehousing and replanning which belong in the main to the twentieth century—a period in London's history which is almost respectable beside the six preceding centuries.

These constants, then, can be seen to have evolved during a period covered broadly by the fourteenth to nineteenth centuries. While they provided a backdrop to London's role as a wicked city, they were parallel to her growth as a major commercial capital.

How did London develop in this Jekyll and Hyde way?

The Romans made London a trading centre more by convenience than design. There may have been a small settlement there at the time of the Roman invasions, but the invaders intended to make the ancient town of Colchester the seat of government. The layout of Roman roads shows that the site of London was at first bypassed. The Essex Stane Street, the modern A120 trunk road, ran due west from Colchester towards the centre of the country. Colchester's road link with London is a spur off this road. Similarly, Watling Street, heading west from the Kent coast, forded the Thames at Westminster before turning northwest, obviously allowing soldiers and supplies to move as quickly as possible to the Celtic frontiers. Fording points and crossroads became important landmarks and in many cases were the positions of settlements.

After the conquest, the Romans required a main base where British hides, grain and timber could be shipped to Gaul. There was only one practical site, on two small hills where the Thames was contained within hard banks. Surrounding the hills was marshy ground and from the northern marsh (which became Moorfields) the Wall Brook flowed between the two hills into the Thames. The centre of Londinium, as the settlement was called, grew into a walled town of 326 acres with seven gates and a population of about 30,000. It was a natural centre of communication for road and sea. The road system expanded and the alignment by Roman engineers of the York road (Ermine Street) with the Chichester road—the other Stane Street—determined the site of London Bridge. The military centres were all to the north and west, so that London's commercial function flourished without restriction.

When the Romans left Britain, trade declined but in 883 the city became a key point once more when it was refortified against the Danes by Alfred with a 'southern bulwark'—the settlement of Southwark. (Southwark itself showed some remarkable character for many centuries as a district for brothels, bear fights and, later, theatrical performances.)

By the Norman conquest, London was in a unique position compared to other European capitals. Not only had it avoided being the seat of government but also it had escaped becoming the headquarters of the Church. The kings ruled their subjects from Westminster and the archbishops controlled matters spiritual from Canterbury. Thus all the interests and talents of Londoners could be freely focussed on trade. True, there were 126 churches in London to care for the 75,000 population during the twelfth century but there was no room to build large palaces or abbeys within the city walls. When William I built the White Tower, he had to site it outside the east city wall. So Londoners could express their opinions and feelings (which they usually did by rioting) with considerable freedom. And away from the immediate influence of church and state, they prospered. It was at this time that the chronicler Froissart commented:

> *The English are the worst people in the world, the most obstinate and presumptious, and of all England the Londoners are the worst . . .*

Mediaeval times saw the beginnings of the Guilds and Companies formed by different trades and the clashes between them, the influx of Flemings, Franks, Venetians, Lombards and Genoese from abroad, and the wild element of apprentices whose high spirits echoed in London streets for the next few hundred years. To the rest of England, London was a lively, rich capital, and this image attracted people from other regions to the city as, indeed, it does today.

Although shipping and the cloth trade were the chief industries, London was starting to acquire the characteristics of an industrial city. There were already squalid slum tenements where light-metal workers lived. Breweries, ironworks and other workshops had begun to pour smoke into the city's atmosphere. New villages with poor, crowded dwellings were developing outside the city and the surrounding boundaries. The problems of overcrowding with their sinister implications had begun.

Two main events in the fourteenth century had an enormous effect on London and on the country as a whole. The Black Death in 1348–49 killed one person in three. This disastrous plague made labour scarce and many landowners found it more profitable to enclose their arable land and raise sheep for the wool trade. Consequently, distressed crowds of labourers wandered around the country looking for work, moving into the cities. The result was appalling poverty in London with a subsequent stimulus to crime. Despite the catastrophe of Black Death, London's population in the fourteenth century rose to 100,000. An Italian visitor to London at the end of the fifteenth century had to say, in spite of the severe laws and the extensive powers of the magistracy,

> ... there is no country in the world where there are so many thieves and robbers as in England; insomuch that few venture to go alone in the country, excepting in the middle of the day, and fewer still in the towns at night, and least of all in London.

In 1517, the numbers of beggars in London was estimated to be 1,000 and by the end of the century, 12,000. Henry VIII had added to these numbers when he dissolved the monasteries because the friars, who had once helped to relieve the poor, now joined the ranks of the poor themselves. Periodically too, discharged soldiers would come to London to look for work. These 'veterans' were all the more dangerous to law and order when they were allowed to keep their arms and uniform to make up deficits in their pay. Right up to the Crimea, soldiers returning from war were to cause trouble in London's streets.

Another form of invasion, which was a regular cause of tension, was the many foreigners who settled in London. The early arrivals came to trade, but more and more, immigrants came to escape Catholic or political persecution in their own countries. An attempt to control overcrowding was made by a proclamation in 1580 which forbade, within three miles of any London gate, the building of any new house where no former house was known to have been within living memory. However, this and other proclamations failed to check the problem. By the end of the century, London had a population of 200,000, with most of the new elements contained in squalid development in Whitechapel, Stepney, Shadwell, Limehouse and Wapping. The violent state of the city is summarised by Thomas Burke in *Streets of London*:

> *Before 1600, with risings and casual riots, and conflicts of natives and foreigners, and daily assaults by thieves and assassins, and frequent executions, there was blood in the London streets almost every week of the year.*

These events, then, shaped the crowded, harrowing conditions which bred the crime, filth and cruelty for which London was infamous in the seventeenth, eighteenth and nineteenth centuries. The conditions reflect in part the attitude of people of the time towards their fellow men, but, as we have seen, are part of the price London had to pay for its prosperity. And during the whole of this latter period, the city's commercial expertise supported the Empire through its most glorious days of conquest, plunder and development.

CHAPTER TWO

ACTS OF GOD

Fog everywhere. Fog up the river, where it flows among green aits and meadows; fog down the river, where it rolls defiled among the tiers of shipping and the waterside pollutions of a great (and dirty) city.

THERE WERE FREQUENT happenings causing terror, calamity and inconvenience in London which were beyond the control of the citizens. All they could do when potential disaster was imminent was to wait fearfully for the interval of panic to pass. One such phenomenon was fog, described here by Dickens in *Bleak House*. Any riverside city can expect fog at certain times of the year, but London became prone to thick bouts as soon as its first coal fires were lit in open grates in mediaeval times.

John Evelyn, the diarist, wrote in 1661:

This horrid smoke obscures our churches and makes our palaces look old. It fouls our clothes and corrupts the waters, so that the very rain and refreshing dews that fall in the several seasons precipitate this impure vapour, which with its black and tenacious quality, spots and contaminates whatever is exposed to it.

Fogs, especially in the last century, concealed many murders and thefts in London and allowed criminals to vanish into murky nowhere. In this way, fog has always been linked with evil, though it took a long time for Londoners to realise that thick fog was less an Act of God than an act of pollution.

Famous London fogs are noted over centuries; two of the very thickest occurred in 1699 and 1772.

Evelyn's diary has this comment on the 1699 fog:

> *There happened this week so thick a mist and fog that people lost their way in the streets, it being so intense that no light of candles or torches yielded any (or but very little) direction. I was in it and in danger. Robberies were committed between the very lights which were fixed between London and Kensington on both sides, and whilst coaches and travellers were passing. It was begun about four in the afternoon, and was quite gone by eight, without any wind to disperse it. At the Thames they beat drums to direct the watermen to make the shore.*

Another well-known fog blanketed the city continually from November 1879 to March 1880. In a more statistical age, the thick fog of December 1952 killed 4,000 people. And some 400 died ten years later during three days of sudden freezing fog. It was a foggy night, too, when ninety people were killed in a train smash at Lewisham in 1957 (the Harrow and Wealdstone disaster of 1952 claimed more dead; 111). The Clean Air Act of 1956 lessened the hold of the traditional 'pea-souper' fogs on the city.

Periodically, too, strong winds blew through London with catastrophic results. *Stow's Annals* note in December, 1599:

> *Yesterday the wind blew west and by south, boisterous and great, where through the tops of many chimneys are overthrown, lead blown off churches, trees and barns blown down. A tilt boat from London going towards Gravesend was lost against Woolwich by wilfulness of the watermen rowing against an anchor: and of 30 persons, men and women, but 11 are saved.*

Samuel Pepys wrote in his diary for February 18th, 1662, that he found:

> *. . . by my walking in the streets, which were every where full of brick-bates and tyles flung down by the extraordinary winde the last night (such as hath not*

been in memory before, unless at the death of the late
Protector), that it was dangerous to go out of doors;
and hearing how several persons had been killed today
by the fall of things in the street . . .

The greatest storm of all for Londoners was in November, 1703, when 8,000 people were killed in southern England. Thomas Burke describes it:

It lasted nine hours. During the night, all the ships in
the river were driven ashore; barges were driven against
the arches of London Bridge and smashed into splinters;
and four hundred of the watermen's wherries were sunk
or broken. Two thousand chimneys were blown down.
Spires and pinnacles of churches crashed to the ground.
The roofs of many houses were whirled off, and in some
parts of the town many houses were uprooted. The lead
on the roofs of the highest buildings was rolled up like
paper, and a score or more night-wanderers were killed
by falling tiles and stones.

It seems that no one had found a way to fasten lead securely on to roofs.

Three centuries later, thousands of people were killed by the fall of other things in the streets—the German bombs of the Second World War. In May, 1941, a night bombing raid killed 1,436 people and injured 1,792.

Far more destructive to morale were the V-2 rockets which fell in the last year of the war. In November, 1944, one killed 174 people when it hit a Woolworth's at New Cross. Another exploded at noon in March, 1945, at the corner of Charterhouse Street and Farringdon Road; over 100 people were killed. Later that month, a V-2 rocket dropped onto two blocks of flats in Stepney and killed 134 people. This was the last bomb to fall on London. The destruction caused by the Blitz (30,000 killed, 50,000 injured, 100,000 houses destroyed, 1,650,000 houses damaged) has no other comparison with London of the past except possibly with the Great Fire of 1666.

In sixteen hundred and sixty-six,
London burnt like rotten sticks.

Fire was a continuous hazard from early days, when Boadicea burned down the young Roman colony in A.D. 60. Houses tended to be built of wattle or wood, with inflammable roofs of straw and stubble. The first St. Paul's Cathedral was burnt out in 961. In 982, the area formerly covered by Roman London was consumed by another fire. St. Paul's was burnt down again in 1087 and a serious fire destroyed wide areas of the city in 1135. The use of stone and tiles cut down on the frequency of fires but crowded conditions within the city walls enabled a blaze to spread quickly. The Great Fire, in a nutshell, according to Bernard Ash in *The Golden City*, destroyed:

> . . . *a city of great squalor, a jerry-built, seething, turbulent anthill of a city. It stank. It was crowded to bursting point.*

The Fire started on the morning of September 2nd, 1666, in Farriner's bakehouse. The broadside ballad *London Mourning in Ashes* describes it:

> *The second of September in the middle time of night,*
> *In Pudding-lane it did begin, to burn and blaze out right;*
> *Where all that gaz'd,*
> *Were so amazed at such a furious flame,*
> *They knew not how,*
> *or what to do that might expel the same.*

~~~~~~

Creed and I did stop at St. Paul's, and in the Convocation-House-Yard did there see the body of Robert Braybrooke, Bishop of London, that died 1404. He fell down in the tomb out of the great church into St. Fayth's this late fire, and is here seen his skeleton with the flesh on; but all tough and dry like a spongy dry leather, or touchwood all upon his bones. His head turned aside. A great man in his time . . .

Pepys's Diary, 12th November, 1666.

~~~~~~

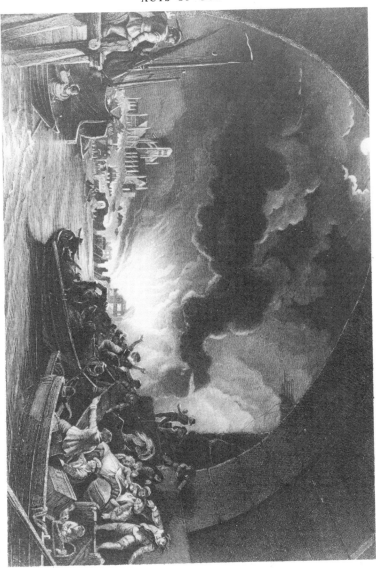

Escape from
the Great
Fire of 1666
—'Under
London
Bridge,
Looking
West' by
A. H. Payne,
after J. de
Louther-
bourg.
RADIO
TIMES
HULTON
PICTURE
LIBRARY

The first casualty in the blaze was the baker's maidservant who was too terrified to crawl along the leads to the next house. After an hour, the Lord Mayor, Sir Thomas Bloodworth, was informed of the fire. 'Pish,' he said before he went back to bed, 'a woman could piss it out.' But Sir Thomas had underestimated the conditions that made the City so vulnerable to fire. A writer under the pseudonym 'Rege Sincers' published a quarto in 1667 outlining some of those conditions:

> . . . the carelessness of a baker, the solitariness of the night, the disposition of old and ruinous buildings, the narrowness of the streets, the abundance of combustible and bituminous matter, the foregoing summer extraordinarily hot and dry, a violent easterly wind, and the want of engines and water, concur as it were to the production of this wonderful conflagration . . .

At one time during the blaze, the citizens of Oxford noticed that the rays of the sun were unusually tinged with red. This was apparently caused by the smoke, driven westward by the wind.

Surprisingly enough, there were very few deaths reported officially as a result of the Fire. The first Bill of Mortality published after the blaze listed just four people 'Burnt at several places'. Pepys saw some of the first casualties; 'the poor pigeons, I perceive, were loth to leave their houses, but hovered about the windows and balconies till they burned their wings and fell down'. William Taswell, a boy at Westminster School (he was to become a clergyman), wrote of the mob's displeasure with Roman Catholics and Frenchmen who were at first alleged to have started the Fire. One Frenchman was felled 'instantly to the ground with an iron bar'. Another Frenchman was 'almost dismembered in Moorfields, because he carried balls of fire in a chest with him, when in truth they were only tennis balls'. Taswell saw one of the first casualties of the Fire:

> I forgot to mention that near the east walls of St. Pauls a human body presented itself to me, parched up as it were with flames, whole as to skin, meagre as to flesh, yellow as to colour. This was an old decrepit woman

*who fled here for safety, imagining the flames would
not have reached her there. Her clothes were burnt,
and every limb reduced to a coal.*

The old woman was one of the few who had preferred to stay
in the City and risk the dangers of the Fire. Most other people
—many thousands, in fact—headed out into the countryside
north of London carrying their goods and camping as best they
could in tents or lean-to sheds. Thomas Vincent in *God's
Terrible Voice in the City*, published in 1667, writes of their
feelings:

> *It would have grieved the heart of an unconcerned
> person, to see the rueful looks, the pale cheeks, the
> tears trickling down from the eyes, the smiting of the
> breast, the wringing of the hands; to hear the sighs and
> groans, the doleful and weeping speeches of the different
> citizens, when they were bringing forth their wives and
> their little ones out of their houses, and sending them
> into the countries, or somewhere into the fields with
> their goods.*

A Royal Declaration and Proclamation commanded local
authorities to see that food and shelter were available to the
refugees. The homeless were panicked at one time by a rumour
that the French and Dutch forces were invading the City. They
seized weapons and left their goods, searching for the invaders.
Guards and troops of soldiers did 'with infinite pains and great
difficulty reduce and appease the people,' wrote Evelyn. It was
Evelyn who described the second day of the Fire in dramatic
terms:

> *God grant my eyes may never behold the like, who now
> saw above ten thousand houses all in one flame, the
> noise and crackling and thunder of the impetuous
> flames, the shrieking of women and children, the hurry
> of people, the fall of towers, houses and churches was
> like a hideous storm, and the air all about so hot and
> inflamed that at the last one was not able to approach
> it . . . London was, but is no more.*

When after blazing for five days, the fire died out, 436 acres had been burned, and 13,200 houses, 89 parish churches, 44 Halls of City Livery Companies and many other buildings destroyed. A half-witted French watchmaker called Hubert who declared that he started the fire was executed as a scapegoat but subsequently it was found that Hubert did not come to London until two days after the blaze started. Pepys watched the Great Fire from the Tower:

> *Every body endeavouring to remove their goods, and flinging into the river, or bringing them into lighters that lay off; poor people staying in their houses as long till the very fire touched them, and then running into boats, or clambering from one pair of stairs by the waterside to another.*

There were other serious fires to follow. Most of Whitehall Palace burnt down in 1698. In 1834, the Palace of Westminster, including the two Houses of Parliament, was burned to the ground. Covent Garden Theatre was devoured by fire twice, in 1808 and 1856. There were several large warehouse fires. The biggest holocaust since 1666 occurred among the warehouses on the South Bank around Tooley Street in 1861. In the year that the Metropolitan Fire Brigade was founded, 1866, a fire at St. Katherine Dock caused two million pounds' worth of damage. But the difference with these latterday fires was that they were confined to public buildings and commercial premises; no longer were there fires which swept away large areas of housing in one conflagration.

In Henry Mayhew's *London Labour and the London Poor*, a table compiled by a fire inspector lists the main causes of fires in London between 1833 and 1849 as

	Average Fires per Annum
Candles, various accidents with	*169*
Flues, foul, defective, etc	*75*
Unknown	*63*
Gas	*46*
Stoves over-heated	*37*
Linen, drying, airing, etc	*30*

Further down the list, other causes included

Children playing with fire or candles	*14*
Lucifer matches	*11*
Suspicious	*7*
Apparel, ignited on the person	*4*
Incautious fumigation	*3*

Once a fire was raging, 'the average duration of time before the fire-brigade, or any parochial or local fire-engine, reached the spot was 36 minutes'. It was a favourable period to be an arsonist, a pyromaniac or even a murderer, if flames had time to destroy vital evidence without being checked.

From flames to ice: every 15 years or so, just as it seems to happen today, a severe winter would hit London. The times of these winters are remembered because the Thames would freeze over. *Stow's Annals* record in 1598:

> *These last days by reason of the great frosts the Thames hath been well-nigh frozen over at London Bridge, but now it beginneth to thaw.*

The key to the freezing of the Thames was London Bridge. When the bridge was rebuilt with wider arches in 1831, the river flowed faster with the result that it has never frozen again. Until 1750, when Westminster Bridge was built, London Bridge was the only means of crossing the river on foot. At times the congestion in the narrow passageway between the buildings on the bridge bordered on the perilous. In 1396, nine people were crushed to death in the rush to welcome a royal procession crossing the Bridge. The *Gentleman's Magazine* in 1749 spoke of a three-hour traffic jam for carriages on the bridge at the time of a concert at Vauxhall Gardens. A feature of the old London Bridge was the row of spikes at the southern end of the bridge on which the heads of criminals were impaled and under which travellers crossing over to London had to pass.

This grisly custom lasted for nearly 400 years. The first recorded reference to it was in 1305, when the head of William Wallace, the great Scottish patriot, was set up on a pole on London Bridge. Not only heads were exhibited there but parts of bodies as well. After Jack Cade's rebellion in 1450, there were so many heads on the Bridge that a temporary ban was placed on the custom.

Among distinguished victims whose heads were shown there were the Earl of Northumberland in 1403 and John Fisher, Bishop of Rochester, and Sir Thomas More, both in 1535. The same pole was used to impale the heads of Fisher and More. Crowds came to see Fisher's head which stayed fresh for a considerable period of time. More's daughter, however, bought her father's head (there was a Bridge officer responsible for the heads) and took it away lest 'it should be food for fishes'. Usually, the heads stayed on the Bridge until they rotted away.

Foreign visitors to London were often fascinated by the sight of the heads. Frederick of Wurtenburg wrote that he counted some 34 heads there in 1592 and the Duke of Stettin noticed 30 heads there ten years later. In 1562, a gruesome use was made of them. Some German workers employed by the Mint were affected by the fumes of molten metal. They were told that a cure was to drink from the skulls of dead men. Accordingly, the Council gave permission for cups to be made from the heads on London Bridge. The Germans drank from these and 'founde some relief, though the mooste of them dyed'. The last head on record to go on show on the Bridge was that of William Stayley in 1678, executed for taking part in the Popish Plot.

Many times, when the Thames was frozen over, enterprising citizens would hold a Frost Fair on the ice. Rows of booths would be set up with food, drink and many amusements. The most famous Frost Fair was the one held in the hard winter of 1683–84, of which several illustrations were made. Other well-known Frost Fairs were held in 1698 and 1715. In 1739, a frost and a strong wind were mixed, causing £100,000 damage to shipping in the river and freezing people to death on both land and sea. Coal became so expensive that the poor could not buy it and suffered accordingly.

In 1768, during the prolonged winter, a shoemaker died of cold in his own stall; very few people had the means to maintain continual heating. The final Frost Fair was held during the Regency period, when the Thames was frozen over for the last time. Booths and side-shows were set up as usual, but a sudden thaw appeared on the fifth day. The ice cracked and gave way. Hundreds of people were thrown in the water and many drowned.

In the same year, eight people were also drowned in a unique accident. A three-thousand gallon beer vat burst in Meux's brewery in Tottenham Court Road, causing other vats to split. Nearly ten thousand gallons of beer poured out of the brewery into areas and cellars of neighbouring St. Giles. When the beer had finally drained away, the bodies of the unfortunate eight were found in the beer-soaked basements.

The threat of an invading army never failed to bring terror to the city. There are many examples. One has been mentioned; the sacking of Londinium by Boadicea, Queen of the Iceni tribe in East Anglia. The consternation and panic in the colony must have been widespread, because Suetonius Paulinus, the Governor of Britain, was forced to leave the citizens to their fate. His main body of troops was still in the Midlands, and he had too few men with him to stand up to thousands of wild British tribesmen. Paulinus was able to defeat Boadicea and her repulsive horde in formal battle later with consolidated forces, but before he could achieve this, virtually everyone in Londinium perished in fire and slaughter.

The repeated plundering of the town by the Danes in the ninth century brought the berserk cruelty of the Vikings, until Alfred fortified the defences. William the Conqueror treated the town in cat-and-mouse style; his troops made a wide sweep of slaughter and arson through the countryside, finishing at Southwark, which they promptly burned. The apprehensive Londoners quickly came out in support of their new masters. Other militant forces also approached London from the south in the centuries which followed. They included the Kentish rebels under Wat Tyler in 1381, the rabble led by Jack Cade in 1450, Lancastrians in 1452 and Cornish rebels in 1497. In 1589, a horde of discharged soldiers, which was threatening London, was scattered by two thousand city militiamen.

In the next century, Spain was a big bogey. The false report of a landing by a second Armada is noted in the State Papers of 1599:

> *Towards evening yesterday came news that the Spaniards are landed in the Isle of Wight and Southampton, which bred unwonted fear and consternation in London, with such a cry of women, chaining*

*of streets and shutting of the gates as though the enemy
had been at Blackwall.*

Holland did better than Spain. A Dutch fleet sailed up the
Medway in June, 1667. Pepys commented:

> *... all our hearts do now ake; for the news is true that
> the Dutch have broke the chaine and burned our ships,
> and particularly* The Royal Charles; *other particulars
> I know not, but it is said to be so. And the truth is I do
> fear so much that the whole kingdom is undone . . .*

Fortunately for London Pepys's fears were unrealised.

The 'March to Finchley' by William Hogarth, 1745.
RADIO TIMES HULTON PICTURE LIBRARY

However, in December, 1688, Dutch infantry actually took possession of Whitehall. The occasion was when James II was deposed in favour of William of Orange. A few days before, an alarming rumour caused 'affrighted crying'. It was reported on the evening of the 12th that thousands of Papist Irish soldiers were advancing on London. Barricades were quickly erected, and no one slept that night until the news was discredited.

Another invasion panic came with the chilling news that Charles Edward Stuart, the Young Pretender, had reached Derby on Black Friday, December 6th, 1745, leading a formidable army of Jacobite Scotsmen. It is said that George II made plans to escape to the continent on hearing this. There was certainly a run on the Bank of England and heavy requisitioning of horses. Hogarth's cartoon 'March to Finchley' shows the chaotic state of a drunken rearguard of a Guards regiment, whose main body is marching off to Scotland at this time—presumably via Derby.

The most serious threat of invasion, if one is to discount Hitler, came from France after the French Revolution and during the Napoleonic Wars. Like Hitler, Napoleon never reached Britain although a handful of French troops came ashore at Fishguard in 1797. London raised a huge force to defend itself. Although these reserve troops were never sent into battle, they were used to preserve law and order when riots broke out during the near-famine situation caused by the shortage of corn at this time.

Most of these tribulations and many other minor ones did not fulfil their potential threats to London's citizens. But in a country which retained superstitions as well as acting against witchcraft well into the eighteenth century, fears of unknown peril could be more horrific and frightening to the imagination than many of the cruel practices and events of everyday London life. If nothing else, a common menace temporarily united the city's society in which even the underworld had clear divisions of class and prestige (for instance, a highwayman outranked a pickpocket). In the same way that modern cities such as Tokyo and San Francisco can be shattered by earthquakes without warning, so London was vulnerable at times to circumstances of chance which nobody within the city boundaries could control.

Dead are removed by night during the London Plague of 1665–1666. *RADIO TIMES HULTON PICTURE LIBRARY*

CHAPTER THREE

PLAGUE AND PESTILENCE

In the evening home to supper; and there to my great
trouble, hear that the plague is come into the City . . .

MR. PEPYS, writing in his diary on June 10th, 1665, and armed
with a bottle of plague-water, survived the next twelve ghastly
months during which 100,000 Londoners died of plague. This
was the last great occurrence of plague that the city was to
suffer. The disease had come to London several times before;
it had first been reported in Britain by the Venerable Bede in
the seventh century.

Whenever epidemic diseases broke out in London, they
thrived on three familiar conditions which had existed ever since
the settlement became a city: overcrowding, filthy sanitary
conditions, and an inadequate water supply for the population.
In 1602, a fresh proclamation restricting new buildings in an
attempt to curb overcrowding justified itself in these terms:

. . . the like orders are again set forth because of the
continual increasing of people in the City which could
hardly be provided of victuals and food and other like
necessaries upon reasonable prices; and especially for
that great multitudes of people being brought to inhabit
small rooms, whereof a great part being very poor and
such as must live by begging or worse means, and being
heaped together and in a sort smothered with many

*families of children and servants in one house, it must
needs follow that if any plague or universal sickness
should by God's permission enter among those multitudes, it would spread itself not only in the confines of
the City but throughout the whole realm.*

But Londoners were either indifferent to making their city
clean and uncrowded, or were unable to do so. Nine years before
the proclamation, Simon Kellway in his *Defensative against the
Plague* had contended that dirty streets and crowded rooms
helped to spread plague and so had recommended that the
streets be 'kept clean and sweet, and cleansed from all filthy
things'. This would have involved constructing a capacious and
efficient water supply for the city. The Thames, by now well
polluted, provided most of London's water (as it does today)
and although a supply of fresh water had been conveyed to the
city since the thirteenth century by conduits from rivers and
springs to the north, access to cisterns and tanks was limited
for most of the population. Many of the conduits, too, were far
from clean at times; in 1597, the old keeper of the conduit near
St. Paul's and an old woman were pilloried because they 'in the
night entered the conduit, washed themselves, and evacuated
their bowels therein'.

Reforms to the water supply came eventually. The Metropolitan Water Act of 1852 made filtration compulsory and the
Metropolitan Water Board which supplies and controls the
water of Greater London was founded in 1902. Today, the
daily consumption per head of water in the 539 square miles
supplied by the Board is about 59 gallons. But as far as sewage
disposal went, a change of attitude was needed just as much as
a change of method. Most Londoners were content to dump
refuse in their rivers, streets, or inadequate drains, and live with
obnoxious sights and smells.

An Inquisition of 1288 determined that the Wall Brook should
be 'made free from dung and other nuisances' but a century
later, the stream was blocked by 'divers filth and dung' thrown
in by people living in houses along the banks. In 1290, the White
Friars whose priory was a hundred yards to the west of the
River Fleet, or Fleet Ditch as it was known, complained that
the stink of the Fleet was stronger than the smell of the incense
they burned and that it had caused the deaths of some brethren.

The state of the streets added to the odours. There was no attempt at any kind of hygiene. People threw all their household refuse into roadways where it became mixed with mud—an evil-smelling combination for pedestrians to plod through. Reinforcing the stench, slaughter houses, tanneries and breweries added their wastes to the streets as well as to the Thames, Wall Brook and the Fleet. From 1309 on, London had ordinances dealing with the disposal of sewage and offal. All these decrees were largely ignored. People continued to build pigsties outside their houses, block gutters with dung, throw dead animals into the rivers and tip rubbish into the public latrines. Many of these latrines were found on platforms above the rivers and at the gates. After the Great Fire, an effort was made in 1674 to turn the Fleet into a canal. The garbage and debris were dredged up and wharves built. But within a few years, the Fleet was choked with rubbish again. Swift and Steele wrote in the *Tatler*:

> *Now from all parts the swelling kennels flow,*
> *And bear their trophies with them as they go:*
> *Filth of all hues and odours seem to tell*
> *What street they sail'd from, by their sight and smell . . .*
> *Sweepings from butchers' stalls, dung, guts and blood,*
> *Drown'd puppies, shaking sprats, all drenched in mud,*
> *Dead cats, and turnip tops, come tumbling down the flood.*

In 1733, the Fleet was covered over and it became an underground sewer. Pope, too, wrote of the Fleet as 'rolling its tributes of dead dogs to the Thames'. It was then left to the Thames to acquire a reputation as one of the dirtiest rivers in Europe. It was nothing more than a vast, open sewer, with every drop of sewage from both banks flowing into it. All the refuse was washed out and in again by the tides, and later, sewer gas from the river became a danger to the men driving the first tunnels under the Thames. In early Victorian times, the colour of the Thames varied between dark green and black. The problem became worse when water closets were introduced. These needed an improved system of liquid household waste disposal. Many people felt sick when they went near the river. During the hot dry summer of 1858, known as the Great Stink, the curtains of the Houses of Parliament had to be soaked in chloride of lime to counteract the repellent odour. The problem was finally overcome when the new Metropolitan Board of Works, formed in 1856, built large, intercepting sewers which crossed London from west to east. All sewage was now carried down this sewer to be emptied in the estuary, and the Thames ceased to smell.

Away from the Thames, the early Victorians tolerated many other foul conditions. Defective drains in both rich and poor districts were often blocked. There were many stinking, over-flowing earth closets. Contents of privies were mixed with ashes and dumped in huge mounds. The thousands of horses pulling vehicles added continually to the piles of dung in the streets. Rats came up from the sewers at night to look for food, often attacking sleeping children. In Bethnal Green, there was a huge artificial lake 230 feet long by 40 feet wide composed entirely of putrefying matter. Charles Kingsley saw people in Bermond-sey in 1849 'with no water to drink but that of the common sewer stagnating under their windows, full of dead fish, cats and dogs'. The water of the Serpentine in Hyde Park was fouled by a sewer until 1860, not before infecting many boating parties.

Mayhew estimated in *London Labour and the London Poor* that the quantity of horse dung dropped in London was about 1,000 tons a week. He quotes a Board of Health report:

Much of the horse dung dropped in the London streets,
under ordinary circumstances, dries and is pulverised,

On the western side of Spitalfields workhouse, and entering from a street called Queen-street, is a nightman's yard. A heap of dung and refuse of every description, about the size of a tolerably large house, lies piled to the left of the yard; to the right is an artificial pond, into which the contents of cesspools are thrown. The contents are allowed to desiccate in the open air; and they are frequently stirred for that purpose. The odour which was given off when the contents were raked up, to give me an assurance that there was nothing so very bad in the alleged nuisance, drove me from the place with the utmost speed.

From a sanitary report by Dr. Hector Gavin, 1848.

and with the common soil is carried into houses as dust, and dirties clothes and furniture. The odour arising from the surface evaporation of the streets when they are wet is chiefly from horse-dung. Susceptible persons often feel this evaporation, after partial wetting, to be highly oppressive. The surface-water discharged into sewers from the streets and roofs of houses is found to contain as much filth as the soil-water from the house-drains.

Despite all these instances of filth, a group of people known as 'toshers' used to roam the sewers looking for coins, cutlery and jewellery which they would find occasionally in the dark, dirty tunnels. The toshers would wander for miles under the streets, carrying a lantern and a stick to defend themselves against rats.

An inquiry into the state of London's sewage system in 1848 drew the following evidence from Dr. Arthur Hassall who had conducted some experiments with London sewer water:

A small fish, placed in a wine glass of sewer-water, immediately gave signs of distress, and, after struggling violently, floated on its side, and would have perished in a few seconds, had it not been removed and placed in fresh water. A bird placed in a glass bell-jar, into which the gas evolved by the sewer-water was allowed to pass, after struggling a good deal, and showing other symptoms of the action of the gas, suddenly fell on its side, and, although immediately removed into fresh air, was found to be dead.*

When asked if he inferred from the experiments that sewer-water, as contained in the Thames near to London, was prejudicial to health, the Doctor declared: 'I would, most decidedly; and regard the Thames in the neighbourhood of the metropolis as nothing less than diluted sewer-water.'

It is not surprising, on considering London's sanitary history, that Londoners were so prone to abhorrent diseases such as

---

* **Henry Mayhew, *London Labour and the London Poor* (1861–62).**

plague, cholera, typhus, smallpox and tuberculosis. Of course, living conditions were similar, if not worse, in other cities. G. M. Trevelyan wrote of the nineteenth century:

> *Not till the seventies did the death-rate decisively fall as a result of building and sanitary reform, and not till the end of the century was sanitation in English cities at all what it should have been.*

So virulent disease was an accepted part of life in London. While it affected the poor in greater proportion, it was a regular visitor to rich households as well. The city's senior diseases, including plague which died out in Britain by 1700, were smallpox, fevers or 'ague' and venereal diseases. Tuberculosis, or 'consumption', as it was called for many years, was widespread in slum areas, too. The Bill of Mortality for December 19th, 1665, lists all the causes of death among the people who died in the city during that year. The biggest killer was, of course, plague but other major illnesses claimed many fatalities:

Ague & Fever	*5257*
Consumption & Tissick	*4808*
Convulsion and Mother	*2036*
Dropsie & Timpany	*1478*
Griping in the Guts	*1288*
Spotted Feaver & Purples	*1929*
Surfet	*1251*
Teeth and Worms	*2614*

Out of the total of 97,306 deaths totalled in the Bill, only 1,545 died from being 'Aged'.

In Tudor times, epileptic convulsion or 'crank' was a favourite sickness for beggars to imitate in order to solicit charity. Such beggars were called counterfeit cranks. Thomas Harman describes counterfeit cranks in his *Caveat for Common Cursitors* in 1566:

> *Many of these do go without writings (testimonials), and will go half naked, and look most piteously. And if any clothes be given them, they immediately sell the*

*same, for wear it they will not, because they will be the
more pitied, and wear filthy cloths on their heads, and
never go without a piece of white soap about them,
which, if they see cause or present gain, they will
privily convey the same into their mouth, and so work
the same there, that they will foam as it were a boar,
and marvellously for a time torment themselves. And
thus they deceive the common people, and gain much.*

But there was no mistaking the distinctive sign of plague.
Buboes, or swelling of the lymph nodes usually in the groin or
armpit, followed shivering, vomiting, splitting headache and
intolerance to light. Once buboes had appeared, the victim had
not long to live.

Plague is a disease that reaches epidemic proportions in
human beings by being passed on by infected rats, or their
fleas. The worst outbreak of plague was the Black Death, the
name given to the pestilence which raged in Europe between
1347 and 1351. The Black Death came originally from Asia and
was brought to Britain by ship in the summer of 1348. It is
estimated that between February and May, 1349, about 50,000
Londoners died; two out of every three. The surviving citizens
had to experience no less than five recurrences by 1400. The
Black Death has been called the greatest disaster experienced
by the western world up to that point. Other years of high
mortality from plague were 1583, 1593, 1603, 1625 and 1636,
but the deaths in London were low in comparison with the
population. For instance, in 1593, 10,675 people died out of the
population of 200,000.

The Plague of 1665 was stimulated by the hot summer of 1664,
during which there had been exceptional swarms of flies, ants
and other insects. The first deaths occurred towards the end of
the year in a slum area which was always receptive to epidemics
—the St. Giles and Drury Lane district. It was in Drury Lane
that Mr. Pepys saw for the first time plague-infected houses with
the customary red cross on their doors together with the words
'Lord have mercy on us'.

The red cross, far from being a symbol of mercy, endorsed
in most cases a death sentence for the entire household. A plague
death in a house meant that all the inhabitants had to be shut
up for forty days' quarantine. Any subsequent deaths in the

house cancelled out the days of isolation; the quarantine had
to begin again with each victim. Information about deaths was
conveyed to the clerks of the parishes by a macabre body of
women called 'searchers of the dead'. The ladies were usually
aged, poor and ignorant. For a small fee, they would 'diligently
search the corps' and report the cause of death. If the cause
was plague, many of the searchers could be bribed to conceal it.
Otherwise, the red crosses were marked on the afflicted houses
and watchmen posted to guard the doors with halberds. The
watchmen were ordered to prevent the inmates from having any
contact with their fellow citizens outside. If the afflicted families
had money, they could persuade the watchmen to buy provisions. Sometimes the watchmen swindled their charges or
nailed up doors and windows to stop the plague victims from
escaping.

Sometimes a family would take desperate action, as James
Leasor writes in *The Plague and The Fire**:

> *Fathers could not bear to watch their families die one
> by one in the stinking atmosphere of a shuttered,
> darkened house, foul with blackened corpses of plague
> victims, the air heavy with the smell of vomit, excreta
> and death. They would creep up to attics with weighted
> ropes and nooses and drop these stealthily over the
> heads of their guards beneath. If the guard still refused
> to unlock the door, they would pull on the rope until he
> changed his mind or was strangled . . .*

Facilities for coping with the victims of plague were never
adequate. At the beginning of the epidemic, the government
authorised the building of some 'hospitals'. These were known
as pesthouses and not one held more than a hundred patients.
The inmates were subjected to gross overcrowding, filth and
lack of medical attention. Most doctors left town, leaving the
sick to be exploited by charlatans with quack medicines and
compounds. While a few brave physicians and apothecaries
remained in London, most medical care of plague sufferers was
carried out by harrowing old women—'plague nurses'—who,
like searchers of the dead, were hired by parishes. Plague nurse

---

* **George Allen & Unwin (1962).**

were sometimes feared more than the plague itself. Not only were they unqualified and 'unwholesome', but also they took every opportunity to steal clothes and possessions from their victims. One doctor who remained in London wrote:

> *What greatly contributed to the loss of the people shut up was the wicked Practices of Nurses. These Wretches, out of Greediness to plunder the Dead, would strangle their Patients, and charge it to the Distemper in their Throats . . .*

As the plague increased, conditions inside plague houses spread to the world outside. The sight of decaying bodies piled on dead carts, the stink of overcrowded graveyards and the silence of the streets, broken by the handbells and cries of the drivers and bearers of the dead cart, became grimly familiar to anyone who stayed in London during the plague. Eventually, a wide area was smitten. The infection spread eastward through the close-packed buildings, through the City and then over the river to Rotherhithe and Deptford. At the height of the plague in August, 1665, Mr. Pepys wrote:

> *. . . The plague having a great increase this week beyond all expectation of almost 2000, making the general Bill*

Most bearers and plague nurses had notorious reputations. One bearer, named Buckingham, would follow his dead-cart, shouting: 'Faggots, faggots! Five for sixpence!' Sometimes he would hold up a dead child by an arm or leg, and wave the tiny, rigid cadaver above his head like a butcher displaying a carcase of meat. When his cart was full and he reached the plague pit, he would lash his torch to a wheel and then go down among the dead and undress the bodies of young women. He was one of several bearers who practised necrophily.

James Leasor, *The Plague and The Fire* (George Allen & Unwin 1962).

(of Mortality) 7000, odd 100; and the plague above 6000. Thus this month ends with great sadness upon the publick, through the greatness of the plague every where through the kingdom almost. In the City died this week 7496, and of them 6102 of the plague. But it is feared that the true number of the dead this week is nearer 10,000; partly from the poor that cannot be taken notice of, through the greatness of the number, and partly from the Quakers and others that will not have any bell rung for them.

Pepys was also disturbed (see Chapter 14) to hear that the churchyards were too full for further burials and that the plague victims had to be buried in open spaces in mass graves. He also noticed that the dead had to be buried by day, because there were more bodies than could be buried at night, which was customary at that time. The plague was finally purged by the Great Fire of the following year.

London Ague was believed to be caused by 'contagions' rising up from marshy ground, and has been described as a type of malaria. London was surrounded by a number of marshes which no doubt contributed to fog and dampness, which in turn aggravated many illnesses. Many distinguished people suffered from London Ague, including Oliver Cromwell and Queen Anne. It has been suggested that the disappearance of London Ague is due to the closing in of the many little streams that used to cross London. Another loathsome disease associated with dampness was Sudor Anglicus, the English sweating sickness, which could manifest itself in epidemics. The treatment for these and other fevers was, more often than not, blood-letting.

In the nineteenth century, tuberculosis, also linked with damp, crowded surroundings, seemed to attack people in their prime; the peak of mortality in women was the 25–29 age group while most male victims were between 30 and 34.

Venereal disease, in the form of gonorrhoea, has dogged civilisation, let alone Londoners, from the earliest times. The origins of syphilis are more obscure. In 1596, a book by Dr. Peter Lowe called *An easy, certain and perfect method to cure and prevent the Spanish sickness* explains that Christopher Columbus brought back the 'great pox' or 'Spanish sickness', as syphilis was known, from the New World in 1492. Modern medical opinion tends to disagree with this explanation. However, venereal disease swept Europe in epidemic form not long after 1493. The etiology of both gonorrhoea and syphilis were not understood until comparatively recently, and quack remedies proliferated for all sufferers. One such sufferer was James Boswell, who caught gonorrhoea unexpectedly from his new mistress Louisa in 1763:

> *I this day began to feel an unaccountable alarm of unexpected evil: a little heat in the members of my body sacred to Cupid, very like a symptom of that distemper with which Venus, when cross, takes it into her head to plague her votaries. But then I had run no risks. I had been with no woman but Louisa; and sure she could not have such a thing . . .**

Boswell broke off the relationship immediately gonorrhoea was confirmed and had to spend five weeks recovering in his rooms, taking various 'medicines' and being bled. His case was far from being exceptional in those days. Venereal disease remained a major problem in London until the twentieth century. In 1856, the situation in London was thus:

> *There were less than three hundred beds in London charity hospitals allotted to venereal patients—including, it seems, the two or three smallish foundations specialising in such cases. Yet three major hospitals (Guy's, St. Bartholomew's, King's College) treated some 30,000 VD cases in the year, and half the surgical out-patients at St. Thomas's fell into this category. VD was rife among merchant seamen and London's situation was presumably aggravated by her enormous maritime trade. Syphilis contracted from sailors from East Asia was especially dreaded for its virulence.†*

A report by a surgeon in 1851 and quoted by Henry Mayhew in *London Labour and the London Poor* contended that one

---

* *Boswell's London Journal*, edited F. A. Pottle (Heinemann).
† *Victorian Underworld* by Kellow Chesney (Temple Smith).

British soldier in five contracted venereal disease every year.

Between 1864 and 1869, Parliament passed the Contagious Diseases Acts which made medical inspections of prostitutes compulsory. While passed in good faith by male politicians in an effort to control venereal disease, female opposition saw the Acts 'as an authoritarian assault on individual liberty'. Eventually, the Acts were suspended in 1883 and repealed three years later.

When Dr. Edward Jenner discovered how to prevent smallpox by vaccination in the late eighteenth century, it meant the control of a disease which almost everyone had at some time in their lives. Not only was smallpox painful, it killed some 2,000 Londoners every year. Survivors from smallpox were left with deep, disfiguring pockmarks in their skins.

Another common disease in London during the seventeenth, eighteenth and nineteenth centuries was typhoid fever. This disease is transmitted by lice among people crowded together in filth and misery, and one repulsive variety was known as gaol fever.

It has been described as:

> *A contagious, putrid, and very pestilential fever, attended with tremblings, twitchings, restlessness, delirium with, in some instances, early phrenzy and lethargy; while the victims break out often into livid pustules and purple spots.**

To this day, judges at the Old Bailey carry posies on the first two days of court sessions and the floor is strewn with herbs to guard against the fumes that were supposed to cause gaol fever. This custom is a reminder that the Old Bailey stands on the site of Newgate Prison. Once, prisoners gave gaol fever to judges, counsel and other people in court who often died as a result. In 1750, sixty people died of Newgate gaol fever, including two judges, the Lord Mayor and several of the jury engaged in the Sessions House. Queen Victoria's rooms at Buckingham Palace were linked to the common sewer and typhus appeared among the Royal family just as it did with many other members of the upper classes.

---

* **Arthur Griffiths, *The Chronicles of Newgate* (1884).**

An alarming disease which confined its worst ravages to the nineteenth century was cholera, the bacilli of which are absorbed through contaminated water. In 1818, word reached England of a new and dire disease which had broken out in India. By 1831, cholera was raging all over Europe, and the Privy Council had issued a warning set of instructions which made the duty of coping with cholera the responsibility of leading citizens in every town and village. The disease came to Britain in October, 1831, and reached London in February, 1832.

The epidemic emphasised the lack of comprehensive sanitary facilities in the city. The violent diarrhoea and vomiting which are the distressing characteristics of cholera make huge demands on water for drinking and washing, and with the water supply so inadequate as it was in the poorer parts of London, the suffering of cholera-afflicted families was appalling. By the summer of 1853, official estimates of cholera deaths were 8,500. There were further outbreaks of cholera in London in 1848 and 1849, when over 13,000 victims died between July and September. Again, the poor districts suffered most—Southwark, Lambeth, Bethnal Green, St. Giles, Rotherhithe. The 1853–54 epidemic was particularly withering in Soho and it was here that Dr. John Snow,* a local doctor, passed into medical history by

---

* The Soho pub, the *John Snow* in Broadwick Street, commemorates the doctor.

‹‹‹‹‹‹‹‹‹‹‹‹‹‹‹‹‹‹‹‹‹‹‹‹‹‹‹‹‹

When these symptoms (diarrhoea and vomiting) ceased, the cramps followed. These constituted the second stage of cholera and began with acute pains, like those of arthritis or rheumatism, in the fingers or toes. They spread up the limbs, and across the chest, often accompanied by a pain in the stomach. At this stage, the patient probably called out in pain and threw himself about in the bed, while his features became collapsed, and his skin turned blue or black. By now he was breathing with difficulty, the air issuing from his mouth with a low whining or moaning sound.

Symptoms of cholera from *King Cholera* by Norman Longmate (Hamish Hamilton 1966).

‹‹‹‹‹‹‹‹‹‹‹‹‹‹‹‹‹‹‹‹‹‹‹‹‹‹‹‹‹

advising that the handle of the Broad Street water pump in the centre of the epidemic area be removed. When this was done, the outbreak in Soho ceased suddenly, confirming in Snow's mind, at least, that cholera was transmitted through water. Ten thousand Londoners died in that third epidemic. In 1866, the last great cholera epidemic in London caused some 6,000 deaths. As there were large demands on hearses, the London Hospital had to hire removal vans from Messrs Pickfords to carry the dead away. However, these outbreaks spurred on large-scale sanitary reform and public health development, and by 1900, cholera was a disease of the past in London.

The cholera bacilli, or vibrios, are so small that as many as 500,000,000 of them can be found in a cubic centimetre of fluid in the intestines of a victim. The vibrios multiply so quickly in their host habitat that soon some of them die of overcrowding, releasing their deadly toxin inside the sufferer.

It is interesting to compare these characteristics with those of London's citizens who themselves multiplied in packed, unhealthy surroundings. The Londoners were fortunate in that they were able to improve their situation before they poisoned themselves and their environment irrevocably.

CHAPTER FOUR

RIOT AND UPRISING

The magistrates of the City of London and the suburbs are warned that certain apprentices and other idle people their adherents, the same that were the authors of the late disorder, have a further purpose on Midsummer evening or night to renew their lewd assembly by colour of the time and to commit a breach of the peace or other foul outrage . . .

So WENT a Privy Council warning to the City of yet another possible riot in the streets. Although this warning appeared in the sixteenth century, it could have been issued two hundred years before or after that time and still be considered a normal event. For rioting was a part of life. It was a spontaneous expression of feeling that could involve hundreds of people in a few moments. The worst aspects were the violence and damage that riots could and did cause. On the other hand, a riot could relieve tension and smouldering resentment. And while a mob in full cry was terrifying to watch, the loss of life, with few exceptions was not high. In an age where human life was accounted cheaply, this fact was perhaps remarkable. Historians, T. H. White for one, have suggested that the British sense of humour prevented more riots from becoming dangerous uprisings than armies of soldiers could. White wrote in his essay *The Mob* which discusses rioting in the eighteenth century:

The interesting feature of the disturbances was that life was seldom lost in them. For the crowd was an English

*one, with a cockney sense of humour, and the voice in
the back row was available, which turned the dangerous
situation to a laugh.*

The eighteenth century has been called the Age of Riots, a
time when serious riots broke out almost weekly. But in proportion to the size of the city, mediaeval riots took place with
exactly the same ferocity. The participants were always the
same kind of people; apprentices, tradespeople and gangs of
young noblemen and squires. Occasionally, an uprising would
take place against an authoritarian grievance. These outbursts,
however, required some form of leadership and were far removed from the localised flare-ups of violence between gangs.
In the thirteenth century, the people of London supported
Simon de Montfort against Henry III and his barons with a
force of 15,000 men.

One frequent cause of resentment among workmen was any
kind of interference in trade by foreigners. If any meddling was
suspected, the situation could touch off a vicious brawl among
those engaged in the trade concerned. Street fights erupted so
regularly that a fourteenth century prohibition banned the
carrying of arms in the streets by anyone except servants of the
king and nobles, and city officials. The prohibition failed to halt
the regularity of street fights. If numbers were required to settle
a quarrel, an instant brawl could be set up with the cry 'Clubs!
Clubs!' Almost immediately, gangs of tradespeople and
apprentices would appear, ready to fight with all kinds of
weapons including knives and the tools of their trades.

One of the earliest instigators of a serious riot in London
was William Fitzosbert, known as Longbeard, whose complaint
was one of the oldest in civilisation. In 1196 he protested against
the heavy taxation imposed by Richard I (largely to finance the
royal ransom from captivity), and declared that it was always
the poor who had to pay for everything. In the ensuing riot,
Longbeard's arrest was ordered by the authorities. He and a few
followers took provisions into the Church of St. Mary-le-Bow,
Cheapside, and prepared for a long siege. There Longbeard
stayed, resisting threats and persuasions, until he and his
companions were smoked out, half suffocated, when lighted
faggots were placed against the church door. They were quickly
dragged through the streets to Tyburn and hanged in the

presence of a large crowd. Many sympathisers carried away pieces of the scaffold and handfuls of the last patch of earth where Longbeard trod as talismans to heal the sick.

Longbeard's uprising took place during Passion Week. Early spring was a traditional time for rioting, particularly among the apprentices. For instance, while a remark and a blow could start a riot at any time, Shrove Tuesday was a day when by custom London apprentices were allowed to 'let off steam'. William FitzStephen in the twelfth century writes how Shrove Tuesday was a time for young men to play at ball games. However, the apprentices would sometimes get out of hand and cause extensive damage to property and sometimes to life. By the early seventeenth century, apprentices on Shrove Tuesday might cause uproar in a theatre and even compel players to act parts which were popular with them. Afterwards, the young brawlers might damage the building and raid nearby bawdy-houses, always a favourite target. The eve of May Day was also a time when apprentices went on the loose. One riot has passed into history as Evil May Day, when a protest was made in 1517 against overbearing foreign craftsmen.

When the Lord Mayor and council heard that an uprising was planned, they ordered all apprentices and servants to stay indoors for twelve hours from nine o'clock on May Day Eve. At the same time, the ringleaders of the uprising were held under lock and key in Newgate Prison and some of their henchmen were sent to the Counter prison in the Poultry. But two apprentices missed hearing the curfew order. They were caught sparring with cudgels by City watchmen and had to call for help with the apprentices' cry. Almost magically, a crowd of friends appeared and rescued them, and the riot went ahead as planned. The leaders were set free and the Lord Mayor's men watched helplessly as the mob plundered and tore down houses where foreigners lived. When the riot was over and authority had gained control again, thirty rioters were sentenced to death for taking part in the disturbance. However, only one was executed. He was John Lincoln, the man who instigated the protest against foreigners.

As adults and qualified workers, apprentices would become members of a guild or company and on many occasions would take part in battles between rival groups. In 1327, some saddlers joined in a fierce and famous battle with a united party of joiners, painters and lorimers. In 1339, the Skinners' Company and the Fishmongers' Company appointed champions to settle a dispute by combat. However, the champions and their body-guards met accidently before the appointed time and soon a large brawl had broken out. When the Lord Mayor and his constables went out to arrest the champions, he was attacked by both the Skinners and Fishmongers and had to be rescued by his sheriffs. The two champions and other ringleaders were arrested, sentenced to death and executed at the Cheapside Standard.

The example of William Fitzosbert was followed in the early fourteenth century when Edward II demanded a forced loan and a troop of soldiers from the City. The citizens refused. The king then deposed the Mayor and put Stapledon, Bishop of Exeter, in charge of London. However, an armed band of citizens managed to obtain the keys of the gates before they were taken away from the Mayor. Then a large mob set fire to the Bishop's house and captured the Bishop himself, who was on horseback, at the north door of St. Paul's Cathedral. Stapledon was dragged to the Cheapside Standard, denounced as a traitor, and be-headed. The Bishop's brother, one of his retainers, and a citizen friendly to the king were beheaded as well. The bodies of all four were dragged through the streets and flung into a ditch at Temple Bar. This outburst was an example of how feelings could be aroused if the monarch made excessive demands on the pockets and freedom of Londoners.

Among the worst troublemakers in London's streets for many centuries were the groups of young men of good family and their retainers. In mediaeval times, their activities were mostly confined to brawling. These gangs tended to roam through the city at night, fighting among themselves, damaging houses and shops and starting fights with local youths. Liveried retainers were also quick to uphold their master's prestige outside his mansion and would start a brawl on the smallest pretext.

One occasion when many apprentices, tradespeople and young squires were united in 'aggro' was during the Peasants' Revolt of 1381 under Wat Tyler of Maidstone. The Revolt, which has been called the 'first pitched battle between Labour and Capital', began when country workers rose against their ex-ploitation by the ruling class and the imposition of the shilling poll tax. The militant Kentish peasants marched to London and were welcomed by the apprentices. Soon the slaughter began. The young King Richard II was blockaded in the Tower and several of his ministers, lawyers and jurors were hunted down and hurried along to be beheaded at Cheapside or on Tower Hill. The Chancellor, Archbishop Simon of Sudbury, was snatched from sanctuary in the Tower and his head was paraded around the streets on a pike. Eventually all the heads were placed on the spikes of London Bridge. The mob also succeeded in looting Lambeth Palace and burning the prisons of Newgate and the Fleet. Earlier, Richard had prevented worse bloodshed at a meeting with the peasants at Mile End where:

> . . . *At the prayer of the infuriated rout, our Lord the King granted that they might take those who were traitors against him, and slay them, wheresoever they might be found.*

The revolt was finally halted at a second conference at Smithfield. While standing beside the King, Wat Tyler brandished a dagger and pulled roughly at the bridle of Richard's horse. In alarm, the Mayor, William Walworth, stabbed Tyler. In the tense situation, Richard saved the day again by declaring himself the leader of the rebels and granting their demands. As Richard led the mob northwards from Smithfield, Tyler was taken to St. Bartholomew's Hospital. However, his stay there as a patient was short. With the mob removed, he was dragged out and beheaded.

Another leader of an uprising who came to an undignified end in London was Perkin Warbeck, pretender to the throne who claimed to be the Duke of York, one of the Princes in the Tower. Warbeck, in 1499, according to a description which appeared in 1610:

> . . . *was set in the stocks at Westminster Hall door a whole day, and so likewise the next day was he set on a scaffold at the standard in Cheapside, with many mocks and revilings cast against him; being now in hold again, by false persuasions and great promises, corrupted his keepers and would have fled away, but his purposes being known, he was at last apprehended, taken, and executed at Tyburn, he and his keepers. And that is the end of Perkin Warbeck.*

Warbeck's uprising did not immediately affect London. Some fifty years before, however, Jack Cade led his followers through Blackheath and set up his headquarters at the White Hart Inn, Southwark. A fierce battle ensued on London Bridge between the rebels and the citizens, which continued all night between flaming houses on the bridge. The fires forced women to leap into the Thames with children in their arms. In Shakespeare's *Henry VI*, the king is told next day:

> *Jack Cade has gotten London Bridge;*
> *The citizens fly and forsake their houses;*
> *The rascal people, thirsting after prey,*
> *Join with the traitor; and they jointly swear*
> *To spoil the city and your royal court.*

Fortunately, the joint enterprise was thwarted by the royal forces. Some of Cade's grievances were directed towards foreigners and he called for money from Lombards and other strangers in London, threatening beheading as a penalty for non-payment.

Southwark featured in another threatening yet abortive uprising when Sir Thomas Wyatt, son of Sir Thomas Wyatt the poet, led more Kentish rebels to attack London in 1553. Wyatt wished to place the young Princess Elizabeth on the throne on hearing that Queen Mary, her sister, was going to marry King Philip II of Spain. When Wyatt and his men reached Southwark, guns from the White Tower fired seven or eight warning shots. All bridges, including the drawbridge on the southern side of London Bridge, were ordered to be broken down for sixteen miles upstream. Wyatt had to go as far as Kingston-on-Thames before he could cross the river by bridge. The rebels then returned to London, but the gates were closed and the inhabitants refused to support them. After that, the rebellion was easily subdued. Wyatt was brought to trial and executed, a 'villain and unhappy traitor'.

In Elizabeth's reign, any event that attracted large crowds was open to trouble. Sometimes sheer numbers of people caused misadventure as at the joustings of the Accession Day celebrations of 1581, when 'many of the beholders, as well men as women, were sore hurt, some maimed, and some killed, by falling of the scaffolds overcharged'. At other times, a hint of trouble or injustice would cause a large crowd to gather immediately. In 1592, a wrongful arrest of a feltmaker's servant by one of the Knight's Marshal's men caused 'great multitudes' to assemble who subsequently provoked 'great disorder'. The riot had to be quelled by the Lord Mayor and his Sheriffs.

> *Please to remember,*
> *The fifth of November,*
> *Gunpowder, treason and plot . . .*

On November 4th, 1605, a perilous uprising was prevented which would have given British history a completely new course. Guy Fawkes, a fanatical Roman Catholic, was arrested in the cellars beneath the House of Lords after a tip-off. Fawkes had planned to blow up both Houses of Parliament when the king was there the next day, opening the new session. Fawkes and his fellow conspirators had hoped to take over the government of the country on hearing that the king, James I, wanted to stay a Protestant. Fawkes was tortured severely, tried and sentenced to death with seven other accomplices. Of all the uprisings which took place around London, this was the only one to acquire an anniversary which is celebrated every year with fire, explosive, and injury.

Fawkes aroused the personal interest of the king who compiled a list of questions to be put to Fawkes in the Tower of London by Sir William Waad, the Lieutenant of the Tower, and his staff of torturers. Fawkes held out for five days against excruciating pain before he broke down and revealed the names of his fellow conspirators. He had just enough strength after being stretched on the rack to scrawl 'Guido', his adopted Christian name, on the deposition. One manuscript history of the plot indicates that Fawkes was first hung by his thumbs before being placed on the rack. Another source contends that Fawkes was also held down naked over a heated stone 'until his flesh seared'.

When Fawkes arrived at Old Palace Yard, hauled on a hurdle, to be executed, he was so weak that he had to be helped up to the top rung of the gallows' ladder. After he had been hanged, drawn and quartered, his head was impaled on a spike at London Bridge, first being parboiled with 'bay-salt and cummin-seed'.

In the seventeenth century, riots continued to be violent but the Stuart kings gave the mob more cause to show their feelings against the monarchy. James I showed what was regarded as disproportionate favour to the Spanish ambassador. The mob reacted by throwing stones and garbage at the diplomat when he appeared on one occasion in the city streets. James threatened the City with martial law but did not carry out the threat. However, Charles I came close to imposing military rule on London when a Dr. Lambe, a friend of the Duke of Buckingham, was mobbed to death by being dragged along by his hair and beaten. The Duke was highly unpopular at the time.

In 1641, the king's popularity had sunk to a low ebb. The City's pro-Puritan artisans shouted anti-Royalist slogans in Westminster while apprentices stormed the Abbey. Very little sympathy was shown by the mob when Charles was beheaded. Little by little, the drive of the mob was beginning to match that of the City's ruling classes instead of being against it. Unfortunately, the Puritan influence during the middle of the century suppressed a great deal of the cheerfulness and high spirits in London life. Even the Restoration failed to bring back the original gaiety that Londoners had shown previously in mind and merrymaking.

As a forerunner to the celebrations of the Restoration, the dissolution of the unpopular Rump Parliament produced wild jubilation in the streets with bonfires burning and people drinking and roasting rumps. Before the dissolution, riots and disorders were frequent. A demonstrator was killed when a large band of apprentices and rioters marched to the House of Commons from the City to demand a new Parliament. Finally, the army under General Monk fell in with the mood of the City and country and ordered the Rump Parliament to resign. Monk kept everyone guessing, as Pepys reports:

> All the world is at a loss to think what Monk will do:
> the City saying he will be for them, and the Parliament
> saying he will be for them.

Pepys also reported various disturbances. He noted the activities of a religiously-minded gang in 1661:

> This morning, news was brought to me to my bedside,

that there had been a great stir in the City this night
by the Fanatiques, who had been up and killed six or
seven men, but all are fled. My Lord Mayor and the
whole City had been in armes, above 40,000 . . .

Playing safe, Pepys got out his sword and pistol for which he
had no powder. Later in his diary, he wrote about a familiar
scene in London through the ages—a fracas between tradespeople:

Great discourse of the fray yesterday in Moorefields,
how the butchers at first did beat the weavers, (between
whom there hath been ever an old competition for
mastery,) but at last the weavers rallied and beat them.
At first the butchers knocked down all for weavers that
had green or blue aprons, till they were fain to pull
them off and put them in their breeches. At last the
butchers were fain to pull off their sleeves, that they
might not be known, and were soundly beaten out of
the field, and some deeply wounded and bruised; till at
last the weavers went out tryumphing, calling £100 for
a butcher.

Pepys also saw London apprentices in action. To the north
of Lincoln's Inn Fields was Whetstone Park which had a group
of brothels. On Shrove Tuesday, 1668, City apprentices set out
to wreck these establishments. The military were summoned to
quell the disturbances. The next day, Pepys wrote:

The Duke of York and all with him this morning were
full of the talk of the prentices, who are not yet put
down, though the guards and militia of the town have
been in armes all this night and the night before; and
the prentices have made fools of them, sometimes by
running from them and flinging stones at them. Some
blood has been spilt, but a great many houses pulled
down . . .

Fourteen years later, another generation of apprentices made
a similar attack on Whetstone Park. Five hundred youths broke
down doors and windows and 'made great spoil of the goods'.

We can take it that the 'goods' refers to the property and not the inmates. The motives for these attacks are not known. Many formidable riots at this time were inspired by a fear of a Papist plot which might overthrow the religious and civil liberties of the country. The man who did most to whip up anti-Catholic hysteria was Titus Oates. About three dozen Catholics were executed on Oates's gruesome accusations. Many others were imprisoned. The height of the fear was when the magistrate Sir Edmondbury Godfrey was found murdered in October, 1678, after receiving a written account from Oates. Next year, on the anniversary of Queen Elizabeth's accession day, 100,000 Protestant zealots marched to Smithfield to burn a dummy Pope with live cats inside him to make him squeal.

All through the reign of James II, a Catholic himself, tension remained high. Oates was found guilty of perjury in 1685 and sentenced to be pilloried, then whipped at the cart's tail from Aldgate to Newgate and in two day's time from Newgate to Tyburn.

No one expected Oates to survive this onerous torture which 'was equivalent to sentencing the man to be flogged to death'. But Oates had incredible strength and stamina, as described by the historian Macaulay:

> *On the day on which Oates was pilloried in Palace-yard, he was mercilessly pelted and ran some risk of being pulled to pieces. But in the City his partisans mustered in great force, raised a riot and upset the pillory. They were, however, unable to rescue their favourite . . . On the following morning he was brought forth to undergo his first flogging. At an early hour an innumerable multitude filled all the Streets from Aldgate to the Old Bailey. The hangman laid on the lash with such unusual severity as showed he had received special instructions. The blood ran down in rivulets. For a time the criminal showed a strange constancy: but at last his stubborn fortitude gave way. His bellowings were frightful to hear. He swooned several times, but the scourge continued to descend. When he was unbound, it seemed that he had borne as much as the human frame can bear without dissolution . . . After an interval of 48 hours, Oates was again brought out of his dungeon.*

**Dead cats
and rubbish
pelt Titus
Oates in the
pillory.**
*RADIO
TIMES
HULTON
PICTURE
LIBRARY*

*He was unable to stand, and it was necessary to drag
him to Tyburn on a sledge. He seemed quite insensible;
and the Tories reported that he had stupefied himself
with strong drink. A person who counted the stripes on
the second day said that there were 1,700.*

At intervals for many years to come, the mob was to flare up
with anti-papist fury.

When the Seven Bishops were acquitted in 1688 (they had
petitioned against James's Declaration of Indulgence which
aimed at creating a new Parliament full of Catholics), the mob
exploded gunpowder, pealed bells, burnt another Pope in effigy
in the streets and assaulted many Catholics. Towards the end
of the year, apprentices sallied nightly against the Catholic
chapels in Lime Street, Bucklersbury and Clerkenwell. After the
news of James's flight in December, 1688, the mob rose and
took possession of the city. All Catholic chapels were burnt
down, houses where suspected papists lived were plundered on
the excuse of seeking arms, and foreign embassies were sacked
where vanished papists were believed to be hiding. Sir Arthur
Bryant writes:

*Afterwards the mob marched past the soldiers, holding
aloft flickering gilt candlesticks in solemn mockery
and plundered popish gewgaws, while thousands of
hooligans, waving oranges on swords and staves, yelled
joyously for the reign of Saturn so miraculously come
again.**

It is interesting to compare this march with those of the
Orange Order which take place in Northern Ireland.

At this time, London's familiar pranksters, young men-about-
town, began to operate in groups which were given names. The
new coffee houses that had sprung up were popular with rich
young men called Hectors, Muns and Scowrers. In the early
eighteenth century, an even rougher and more dangerous group
appeared, named after the Red Indian tribe of Mohawks. The
Mohocks, as they were called, made many cowardly attacks at
random after dark. They assaulted watchmen, attacked un-

---

* **Samuel Pepys,** *The Saviour of the Navy* **(Collins 1938).**

protected women such as maidservants and prostitutes, drove swords through the sides of sedan chairs and slit men's noses with razors. Lady Strafford wrote in 1712:

> *I am very much frighted with the fyer, but much more with a gang of Devils that call themselves Mohocks; they put an old woman into a hogshead and rooled her down a hill, they cut some nosis, others hands, and several barbarass tricks, without any provocation. They are said to be young gentlemen, they never take any money from any; instead of setting fifty pound upon the head of a highwayman, sure they would doe much better to sett a hundred on thear heads.*

The Government did in fact offer £100 reward for the arrest of any Mohock. But the Mohocks, in company with their contemporaries the Nickers and, later, the Bold Bucks (gangs who were concerned mostly with young girls), were members of rich families who could buy their sons or nephews out of trouble. Very few Mohocks ever found themselves in serious trouble with the law.

Interspersed among the usual street brawls, riots of many causes in the eighteenth century showed that the populace were quick to register their resentment at any restrictive official or commercial action. Among the riots that took place were High Church Riots, Riots about Admirals, Corn Riots, Election Riots, Tea Riots, Weavers' Riots, Club Riots and, as we have seen, No Popery Riots.

As an example, the Mug House Riots in the early half of the century took place around the Whig tavern club in Salisbury Court. The members became so noisy over their drinking that a crowd gathered outside. After an exchange of insults, the crowd attacked the building and virtually besieged it. Soon the crowd lost interest and dispersed. But later, to the landlord's alarm, a more aggressive mob reformed and approached the house, intent on plunder. The landlord produced a blunderbuss and threatened to fire it if the crowd came close to the house. Which he did when the rioters continued to advance. The leader, a young apprentice, was killed. The crowd attacked the house, burning all the furniture. The Mayor and Sheriffs ordered the crowd to disperse. On their refusal, the Riot Act was read, but still the crowd defied the order. A troop of soldiers was summoned from Westminster, who charged the crowd, scattered them, and seized five people at random. The landlord was tried for murder and found guilty only of manslaughter. The unfortunate five, however, were sent to Tyburn and hanged.

Drink was the cause of more widespread disturbances, the Gin Riots. These occurred when the Licensing Act of 1751 threatened to make gin less easy to obtain. Introduced into England in 1725, gin helped the populace forget their misery and squalor. Large distilleries were built in Clerkenwell, a district which offered supplies of water and grain, ample labour, and a thirsty market. The poor could buy gin almost anywhere; it was estimated by 1743 that one house in eight sold 'Blue Ruin'. Gin was sold in prisons, brothels, barber shops and factories as well as in the streets or privately. The consumption per head in London including children was nearly two pints a week, or a total of eight million gallons a year. The result was debauchery on a mass scale, particularly in the slum areas of Bethnal Green, Westminster and St. Giles, which is the scene of Hogarth's famous picture:

> *Gin, cursed Fiend, with Fury fraught,*
> *Makes human Race a Prey;*
> *It enters by a deadly Draught,*
> *And steals our Life away.*
>
> *Virtue and Truth, driv'n to Despair,*
> *Its Rage compells to fly,*
> *But cherishes, with hellish care,*
> *Theft, Murder, Perjury.*
>
> *Damn'd Cup! that on the Vitals preys,*
> *That liquid Fire contains;*
> *Which Madness to the Heart conveys,*
> *And rolls it thro' the veins.*

Rows of drunken bodies, lying down, propped up by day and night in a kind of continuous orgy, as well as the resulting disorders forced the Government to restrict the sales of gin. The 1751 Licensing Act was so unpopular that riots broke out in all parts of London. Troops patrolled the streets and detachments of the Guards camped in Hyde Park and in Covent Garden.

Fires were started and the mob smashed windows, including those in houses of members of Parliament. The cry of the mob was 'No Gin, No King!' But no one was killed and the soldiers kept firm control of the crowds.

Two riots in which lives were lost were the Spitalfields Silk Weavers' Riot and the Wages Riot, both of which involved weavers. The former riot began as a wages dispute when cheap imported calico undercut many of the prices of the weavers' products. The weavers attacked women and girls wearing calico by throwing acid on their clothes or tearing off gowns. Soldiers were called in and they quelled the rioters promptly by firing on them and killing five. The Wages Riot started when some weavers' employers undercut the agreed standard rate by a penny or so. In their rage, the workers destroyed the looms of these masters and then insisted that all owners of looms should contribute to a Weavers' Fund at the rate of four shillings a loom. The contributions had to be taken to the Dolphin, Cock Lane, but one loom-master took a demand-note to the magistrates. With a search warrant, a party of police and soldiers entered the Dolphin. They were immediately fired on, and one soldier was killed instantly. The racketeers ran, but four of them were arrested and hanged.

The mob took up the cause of the rights of the individual and the freedom of the press when they supported John Wilkes, M.P. for Aylesbury, and the City Aldermen against the King and Parliament. When Wilkes was flung into the Tower in 1763 for attacking the King's speech in his pamphlet *North Briton*, when he was expelled from the House of Commons, and when Sir Brass Crosby, the Lord Mayor, and Alderman Oliver were committed to the Tower, the mob howled their disapproval. Crosby and Oliver, who sat on the magistrates' bench with Wilkes, had freed a printer who had been accused of a breach of parliamentary privilege by printing accounts of debates in the House.

The offending *North Briton*, No. 45, was ordered to be burnt by the common hangman in front of the Royal Exchange. The occasion was a remarkable one. A small bonfire was lit, ready to receive the *North Briton*. Taking a copy, Thomas Turlis, the hangman, approached the fire. Then the mob boiled over in rage. It pelted all the officials present with 'showers of dirt'. The windows of the Sheriff's coach were smashed and he

himself was wounded. Although covered from head to foot
with filth, Turlis managed to thrust the *North Briton* into the
fire. It was quickly rescued by a workman. The hangman and
the escorting constables were put to flight. Realising that the
mob might kill him, Turlis took refuge in the Mansion House.
At one time, angry rioters beheaded members of the Government
in effigy on Tower Hill. On another occasion, they took the
Austrian Ambassador from his coach and chalked '45' (the
number of the offending *North Briton*) on the soles of his shoes.
As usual, the military were called out when the tempers of the
citizens ran dangerously high.

Wilkes himself as a magistrate had to send for soldiers during
the time of the most serious riots since Wyatt's Rebellion—the
Gordon Riots. These riots of 1780 were 'No Popery' in name
but were an expression of unease with their lot by the working
classes. Lord George Gordon, the leader of the Protestant
Association (he wanted to prevent Parliament from lifting
restrictions which banned Roman Catholics from many activities
in public life), aroused more than religious prejudices. On June
2nd, a large crowd gathered under Gordon in St. George's Fields
where the Imperial War Museum now stands. The crowd moved
on to Westminster and surged around the lobbies of the House
while Gordon presented his petition. Outside, the mob, as the
crowd had become, pelted members of the House of Lords with
dirt. Next day, looting and burning began. Mansions were
stormed or burned, gaols were broken open, and houses, chapels
and business premises of Roman Catholics attacked. Gin and
rum from plundered distilleries inflamed the rioters. At Lang-
dale's distillery, at least twenty people drank themselves to death
while the building went up in flames. A beer-wagon driver
mounted on a dray horse led a mob against the Bank of
England at midnight. The staff, with the aid of City volunteers,
beat off the attacks. On the 8th June, the King threatened to
lead troops into the City personally so at last the authorities
allowed some twenty thousand soldiers to tackle the rioters.
Law and order were restored after the troops had killed 285
people. Twenty-nine people were hanged. The total death roll
was estimated to be between 700 and 850.

Not long after the Gordon Riots, the ingredients and character of the mob changed. Business premises were now replacing
more and more of the buildings close to the City where the

members of the mob—the manual workers and the unskilled—lived. There was nowhere the poor could go, except into the detached slum areas circling London where contact with traditional City life was lost. The City, too, lost something. It lost its boisterous atmosphere, its close relationship between governors and governed. Furthermore, a new faceless, unresponsive class was springing up between the mob and the City fathers—the clerks, a race more vital to commerce than the artisans. The days of spontaneous reaction by the mob to different causes were over. Bernard Ash describes the change:

> Hard as life had been in former times, it had the compensation of community, a remote share in the turmoil and the glamour of the Golden City that had made fellows of the great and the lowly. In times of crisis there had been causes to riot over, battle-cries to take up and echo in the roars of the mob. In festal times and times of rejoicing there had been free drink and victuals and merrymaking to share. In the worst of times there had been the saving hand of charity. Now there would be nothing, in a generation that would lose touch with the last vestiges of the paternalism that could make life just tolerable, however hard.

But the nineteenth century had its moments. There were new causes to sing about and some of them, isolated in the drabness of the age following the Industrial Revolution, aroused familiar emotions. Within six months in 1808–9, Covent Garden Theatre and Drury Lane Theatre were burned down. When Covent Garden was rebuilt, Kemble, the manager, raised the prices of the seats to help meet the building costs. The public objected and began a three-month series of riots called the O.P. (Old Price) Riots. They invaded the theatre at every performance and demanded that the old prices be restored. They assaulted the box-office staff and broke the windows of Kemble's house. Finally, Kemble gave in and restored the original prices.

But no local riot could deal with the tribulations of the poor in the war with Napoleon's France. Within two years of the start of the war, there were famine and riot in London. The price of corn rose so high (the penny loaf of bread increased to twopence) that there were crowds of hungry poor clamouring in bread riots. And the population of London was steadily increasing; by the end of the war, there were a million people in a society that was wretchedly harsh towards its poor, especially where working and living conditions were concerned. The situation was aggravated by a flow into the city by large numbers of workers displaced by agricultural and industrial unemployment and by ex-soldiers and sailors discharged by the government into civilian life without any resettlement arrangements. No wonder the first stirrings of radicalism and unionism began at this time.

As we have seen, the authorities by now had means to control disturbances with their own militia forces, and this control was exercised at the riot at Spa Fields, Bermondsey, in 1816. A huge crowd of destitute and displaced people was broken up easily without the help of regular soldiers and so was a later invasion of the Royal Exchange. Four years later, a man who had addressed the crowd at Spa Fields, Arthur Thistlewood, led a group of men in the Cato Street Conspiracy. Thistlewood wanted a revolution and republic similar to that of France and conceived several unsuccessful plans to bring about a new regime in Britain. His last attempt was to plan the murders of the Prime Minister, Lord Castlereagh, and his whole Cabinet. Just before the gang set out from a stable in Cato Street, off the Edgware Road, a Bow Street Runner named George Ruthven pounced on them. Thistlewood was captured next day after killing a police officer and was eventually hanged at Newgate with four colleagues.

The execution of the Cato Street conspirators was the last occasion that men sentenced for treason were decapitated after being hanged. The grisly custom derived from the old sentence for treason of hanging, drawing and quartering. The spectators saw a row of coffins lined beneath the gallows for the conspirators, who showed 'undaunted courage, tinged in most instances with bravado'. Then, when the five bodies had been hanging for half an hour, a masked man (believed to be James Botting, the hangman) came forth to cut their heads off and display them to the crowd. When the first head was held up, the spectators gasped with horror. But by the time that the fifth head went on show, the crowd was laughing at the sight.

During this time, almost as comic relief, London had to put up with the continued antics of the Bucks, young men whose frivolous activities echoed those of the Mohocks. The Bucks, as their predecessors had done, roamed the streets noisily in packs. They performed rowdy pranks such as breaking windows, nailing watchmen in their boxes or cutting traces of coaches to let horses loose. The Bucks frequented much the same area as any group of young men might do today on an evening out in the West End; this lay between Piccadilly and Drury Lane. The activities of the Bucks generally took place between midnight and dawn and were based on several favourite haunts for drinking, gaming and women. These were well-known taverns such as the Royal Saloon, Piccadilly, the Brydges Street Saloon in Covent Garden and the Castle, Holborn.

With the cry for electoral reform growing stronger, outbreaks of disorder were occurring in the big cities. In London, the disturbances were confined to loud, vocal demonstrations, the crowds being controlled effectively by Sir Robert Peel's new police force. For the last time, the London mob agitated on behalf of democracy and occasionally showed its old character-istics. The great Duke of Wellington as Tory Prime Minister of the previous government had opposed the idea of parliamentary reform. When the second Reform Bill was introduced un-successfully by the succeeding Whig government, a mob pelted Wellington on his way home to Apsley House, which had its windows broken by other rioters. The Duke was forced to put up iron shutters.

Charles Greville commented on the situation in his journal on November 10th, 1830:

> It was expected last night that there would be a great riot, and preparations were made to meet it. Troops were called up to London, and a large body of civil power put in motion. People had come in from the country in the morning, and everything indicated a disturbance. After dinner I walked out to see how things were going on. There was little mob in the west end of the town, and in New Street, Spring Gardens, a large body of the new police was drawn up in three divisions, ready to be employed if wanted. The Duke of Wellington expected Apsley House to be attacked, and made preparations accordingly . . . One of the policemen said that there had been a smart brush near

*Temple Bar, where a body of weavers with iron crows
and a banner had been dispersed by the police, and the
banner taken . . . The attack in Downing Street the
night before last turned out to be nothing at all. The
mob came there from Carlile's lecture, but the sentry
stopped them near the Foreign Office; the police took
them in flank, and they all ran away.*

Twelve years previously, Greville had reported much more
dangerous scenes:

*The elections are carried on with great violence, and
every day we hear of fresh contests being in agitation.
The disgraceful scenes which have taken place in
Westminster excite universal shame and indignation.
The mob seem to have shaken off the feelings and the
usual character of Englishmen, and in the brutal attacks
which they have made on Captain Maxwell have
displayed the savage ferocity which marked the mobs
of Paris in the worst times. He has been so much hurt
that his life is now in danger.*

The persistent unrest of the lower classes on behalf of reform
made many members of the House of Lords fear that a French-
style revolution could happen. Finally, the Lords gave way and
the Reform Bill was passed in 1832 amid great rejoicing.

From now on, major threats to peace in the London streets
would come from political groups with few roots in the City.
An example of such a threat was when the National Political
Union of Working People broke a ban and held a militant and
crowded meeting at Calthorpe Street, behind Cold Bath Fields
Prison (near Mount Pleasant). The meeting among the union
members would have probably been quite harmless, but the
imposition and subsequent breaking of the ban attracted not
only thousands of spectators but two thousand police and a
group of officials which included the Home Secretary, two
Commissioners of Police and several magistrates. After two
speeches, both in unprovocative terms, one hundred and fifty
working men marched into Calthorpe Street carrying placards
bearing political slogans. This procession encouraged the police
to break up the meeting with batons. In the ensuing fight, one

policeman was killed, three others were stabbed seriously, and some other constables were hurt by stones. At the inquest on the dead policeman, it was made clear that there would have been no riot if the police had not been there. It took several years before relations between police and public were restored to a completely friendly basis.

In order to combat what might have been a revolution in 1848, a hundred and seventy thousand special constables were sworn in and troops alerted when the Chartists declared that they were marching to Westminster to present a petition. The Chartists were a union of the London Working Men's Association and the Birmingham Political Union. They drew up a People's Charter demanding an annual parliament, manhood suffrage, vote by ballot, abolition of the property qualification for M.P.s, payment for M.P.s, and equal electoral districts. The Chartists announced that they had five million signatures to the Charter and five hundred thousand members were expected in London. However, when the Chartists met on Kennington Common, there were only thirty thousand of them. They were forbidden to march but the petition was permitted to be driven to Westminster in three hackney-cabs. When the petition was examined, less than half the number of signatures claimed were found, and many of them were obviously false as they included the names of Queen Victoria and Punch. A worrying threat to law and order had dissolved into farce. Chartism soon disappeared as trade unionism grew with the co-operative movement and factory reform.

What became a typical method of warfare for Irish insurgents took place in 1867 when members of the Irish Fenian movement tried to free two of their number from Clerkenwell Gaol with explosive. The Fenians attempted to blast down the prison wall. In the explosion, 12 people were killed, more than a hundred injured seriously, and a whole street of houses wrecked. This attack lost the Fenians public sympathy but convinced many politicians that the Irish grievances of the time must be very real. One Fenian convicted of the deed, Michael Barrett (described as 'handsome and young'), went into the history of capital punishment. He was the last person to be hanged in public in Britain.

The Fenians struck again in 1883, mounting a campaign of violence to achieve Irish independence by throwing the administration of the government into utter chaos. The campaign lasted two years, and began in March with the planting of bombs on the same day at the offices of *The Times* and at the Government buildings in King Charles Street, Westminster.

A nightwatchman saved *The Times* from disaster when he bravely picked up a smoking object and laid it in a bucket of water. But the Government offices did not escape. A violent explosion not only wrecked the building where the bomb had been placed but broke most of the windows in buildings in nearby Parliament Street. As this blast also occurred at night, the offices were empty and no one was killed or injured.

A huge crowd gathered, many from the Houses of Parliament, including Ministers, M.P.s, and the entire Press Gallery. In the investigation that followed, the police were able to arrest six men, four of whom were sent to penal servitude for life.

Seven months later, on October 30th, the Fenians left bombs on the underground railway between Westminster and Charing Cross stations and at Praed Street, Paddington. In 1884, the termini of the major railways were chosen as targets. On May 30th, the Fenians tried to blow up Nelson's column in Trafalgar Square, but the fuse attached to 16 sticks of dynamite was defective. On the same evening, Scotland Yard itself was attacked, as was the Junior Carlton Club. The Yard was extensively damaged, with part of the outer wall blown in. Every window in the neighbourhood of the Junior Carlton was shattered. Fortunately, no one was killed or injured.

The south end of London Bridge was attacked on December 13th, while City workers were going home. Most people on the bridge were knocked off their feet by the explosion, and horses bolted in terror. No one was hurt, and the damage to the bridge was negligible. The bomb could have been, according to one theory, 'a very skilfully constructed torpedo of tremendous potency'. On January 2nd, 1885, Gower Street Underground station (now Euston Square station) was attacked with no casualties and very little damage. Three weeks later, three explosions took place on the same day at the Tower of London, Westminster Hall and the crypt of the House of Commons. Sixteen people were injured at the Tower, and two policemen were hurt in the crypt which had a large hole blown in it. A third policeman won the Albert Medal for removing a smoking parcel from the scene.

The Fenian campaign ceased suddenly after that, but the Special Branch formed by Scotland Yard to cope with the Fenians was retained. This was fortunate for London because at the end of the century two other bodies embarked on a reign of terror in Europe. These were the Anarchists, with roots in Italy, and the Nihilists, with Russian origins. These groups operated in France, Spain, Italy and, to a small extent, in Britain.

The Anarchists were the greater threat of the two, but the Special Branch were able to follow their movements through a network of paid informers. Two Italian Anarchists attempted to blow up the Stock Exchange in 1894 but were arrested in time. Another Anarchist was killed in the same year attempting to blow up the Greenwich Observatory. By the next year, Anarchists and Nihilists were no longer a threat to the peace.

In the same year as the Clerkenwell explosion, the first volume of *Das Kapital* by Karl Marx was published. This work stimulated the founding of several societies for political thought and action. H. M. Hyndman, the founder of the Social Democratic Federation, called for results by actions, and many large towns were scenes of outbreaks and demonstrations. In 1886, a year of great social unrest, Hyndman and John Burns led a large crowd of unemployed into the West End to draw attention to their plight. After a meeting in Trafalgar Square, three thousand people detached themselves from the crowd and moved towards Hyde Park. Some of the rowdier members of this section began to break windows in houses and shops along their route. The Carlton Club, for instance, had paving stones tossed through its windows. South Audley Street suffered particularly, as the mob made their way up to Oxford Street. After a day of destruction and looting, sixteen constables confronted an excited crowd of several hundred people. Drawing their truncheons, the policemen courageously charged the gathering which immediately dispersed and fled. However, the unrest continued. Two days later, a rumour that fifty thousand toughs were marching on the West End caused widespread panic, and jewellers and shopkeepers suspended business and barricaded their windows. The threat never materialised. Throughout the next two years, the unemployed were seen many times in fashionable areas. On Sundays, many churches were picketed by the poor, carrying banners to draw attention to their plight.

In November, 1887, came 'Bloody Sunday'. A huge crowd of unemployed estimated at 20,000 held a meeting in Trafalgar Square. To oppose them, a force of 4,000 policemen with a battalion of Guards and two squadrons of Life Guards were drawn up. Three hundred Grenadiers armed with fixed bayonets and ball cartridges lined up in front of the National Gallery. After the clashes, two demonstrators died and two hundred needed hospital treatment. The police earned a great deal of hatred from working-class Londoners which was slow to fade.

London has never been the locale of gang warfare with fire-arms as is often depicted of American cities on film. But in 1910, a battle took place which was more suited to the pages of a spy-thriller than to a winter day in the streets of east London. The affair was the siege of Sidney Street, in which Winston Churchill was involved. On the night of December 16, 1910, a policeman heard movement in a jeweller's shop in Hounds-ditch. A body of police then went to the side door of the building next to the jeweller's and knocked. When the door was opened, the police moved forward. Then a man fired revolver shots from the dark of the doorway and dashed out shooting. Two sergeants and a constable were killed instantly and two other policemen were severely wounded. The gunman and his two companions escaped. Inside the building, tools for boring into the jeweller's shop were found. Next day, a local doctor was asked by two foreign women to visit an injured man at a house off Commercial Road. The doctor found that the man had a bullet wound in his back. When he returned later, the doctor found his patient dead. He reported to the police that he had met two men of foreign appearance leaving the house.

The police searched the area and made several arrests. The man they wanted most was called Peter Piatkow, known as Peter the Painter, a man of Russian extraction. Since 1905, especially after the attempted revolution in Russia, many Russian immigrants had settled in the area. Seventeen days after the murders, detectives heard that Piatkow and a man known as 'Fritz' were hiding in a house at Sidney Street, between Commercial Road and Whitechapel Road. On the 3rd January, an armed band of police besieged the house in front and behind. Winston Churchill, who was Home Secretary, ordered a detach-

Winston Churchill, then Home Secretary, joins Guardsmen and police at the Sidney Street Siege.

ment of Guards to help the police. Churchill himself went to Sidney Street, and a well-known photograph taken at the time shows him examining the situation. Shots were exchanged for five hours. Then the besieged men terminated the siege by setting the house on fire. They continued to shoot while the house was burning over them. The shooting ended when the roof fell in after an hour and a half. Just before that point, the men shot themselves. When the flames were put out, the bodies and wreckage were so charred that no one could make a positive identification of the men, or link them with the Houndsditch murders. There was also no evidence to link the gunmen with any foreign or extremist conspiracy.

Just as in early days, foreigners were involved in a disturbance in the streets of London. But there was no question of a wheel turning full circle. As we have seen, the compact, almost family feeling which had linked citizens of all classes had been broken long ago. The brawls of the mob once had good-natured elements in them, elements of what could be called team spirit or even sportsmanship. But the pressures of commercial development not only drove members of the mob outwards from the City, but also depressed their humour and *joie de vivre*. With the rapid growth of industry, the former benevolence of the masters towards their workers turned into exploitation, and the social divisions between the classes soon cracked deep. Appalling conditions of work and living, indifference to poverty and apathy to improvement were among the worst results. Only towards the middle of the nineteenth century did a public conscience awake to the plight of the poor, and only then did social and municipal reform make practical progress.

Did enfranchisement, better conditions and education prevent the riff-raff of London from emulating the French before them and the Russians after them from rising up in anger and bloodshed to dispose of the means and system of government? Perhaps—but the real salvation of London was the age-old tolerance of its working people, a tolerance which helped to prevent many resentments against society from escalating into catastrophe.

In the twentieth century, the actions of several other politically-motivated groups against law and order caused concern in London. For example, the heirs to the Fenians, the Sinn Feiners, assassinated Field Marshal Sir Henry Wilson, Chief of the

Imperial General Staff, at his front door in Eaton Place on June 23rd, 1922. Two policemen were severely wounded before the two gunmen were arrested. The two assassins, Reginald Dunn and Joseph Sullivan, were convicted and hanged.

From 1925 on, Scotland Yard has been engaged at intervals in checking activities inspired or sponsored by the Soviet Union. More recently, in 1972, four members of the Angry Brigade were convicted for conspiring to cause explosions. The Angry Brigade planted 25 bombs (only six failed to explode) at targets which included the homes of Mr. Robert Carr, then Secretary of State for Employment; Mr. John Davies, then Secretary of State for Trade and Industry, and Mr. William Batty, managing director of the Ford Motor Company. In the same year, Arab terrorists began a campaign of sending letter-bombs to selected Jewish firms and individuals in London. In March, 1973, two bomb explosions—one in Whitehall and one outside the Old Bailey—injured 100 people. One man injured by the Old Bailey blast died later from a heart attack. All these bombs proved that the individual Londoner can still come face to face with shattering violence in modern times. Student riots, demonstrations, bank raids—these could also be included among further threats to peace and safety today.

But no one ever succeeded in persuading Londoners to overthrow authority, not even Jack Cade, who promised his followers in *Henry VI*:

> *. . . There shall be in England seven halfpenny loaves sold for a penny: the three-hooped pot shall have ten hoops; and I will make it felony to drink small beer: all the realm shall be in common . . . there shall be no money; all shall eat and drink on my score.*

CHAPTER FIVE

BEGGARMEN, THIEVES

*April 30th, 1552: The same day was sessions at
Newgate for thieves, and a cutpurse specially was one
James Ellis, the great pickpurse and cutpurse that ever
was arraigned, for there never was a prison and the
Tower but he had been in them . . .*

JAMES ELLIS, famous as a pickpocket, ended up on the gallows
at Tyburn in July. He must have narrowly escaped the gallows
many times before because at this time, three or four hundred
vagabonds and rogues were hanged each year. While there
always have been pickpockets, or foists, as the Elizabethans
called them, at work in London streets, the period saw an
exceptional rise in the numbers of vagrants and thus thieves.

In the street life of mediaeval London shared by courtiers
and cutpurses, knights and knaves, crime flourished in much
the same way as it does today. There were minor activities such
as petty theft, shoplifting, cardsharping and confidence tricks.
There were the more serious ones such as fraud, protection
rackets and armed robbery. Clothes could be stolen off a
victim's back, according to *London Likpenny* by John Lydgate:

> *Then into Cornhill anon I rode,*
> *Where was much stolen gere amonge;*
> *I saw where honge myne owne hoode,*
> *That I had lost amonge the thronge;*
> *To by my own hood I thought it wronge,*
> *I knew it well as I dyd my crede;*
> *But for lack of money I could not spede.*

But in the sixteenth century, economic troubles arising from civil wars and depopulation or rural areas, caused widespread poverty. As a result, thousands of discharged soldiers, unemployed peasants and a large number of 'Egyptians', or gypsies, roamed the land. Many of them were ideal recruits to crime in the big cities. At the same time, the vagrants were chivvied whenever possible, and prevented from settling down in large numbers. In London and Middlesex, there were 'privy searches' at intervals to round up rogues, beggars and vagrants, the wanted men being imprisoned or hanged. Nationally, some 13,000 men were reported to have been arrested in 1569.

Literature of the period defines each kind of thief in detail. In *The Fraternity of Vagabonds* by John Awdeley, there is a glossary of vagabonds, containing names such as Ruffler, Queer-bird, Frater and Abram-man. According to Awdeley:

> An abram-man *is he that walketh bare-armed, and bare-legged, and feigneth himself mad, and carryeth a pack of wool, or a stick with bacon on it, or suchlike toy, and nameth himself Poor Tom.*

> A ruffler *goeth with a weapon to seek service, saying he hath been a servitor in the wars, and beggeth for his relief. But his chiefest trade is to rob poor wayfaring men and market women.*

> A frater *goeth with a like licence to be for some spital-house of hospital. Their prey is commonly upon poor women as they go and come to the markets.*

> A queer-bird *is one that came lately out of prison and goeth to seek service. He is commonly a stealer of horses, which they term a prigger of palfreys.*

Other common names for members of the underworld were cony-catcher (card-sharp), upright-man (superior thief), cross-biter (trickster) and cursitor (vagabond). The first two would require training and practice as would a foist:

> There was a school-house set up to learn young boys to cut purses. There were hung up two devices; the one was a pocket, the other a purse. The pocket had in it

*certain counters and was hung about with hawks' bells
and over the top did hang a little sacring bell; and he
that could take out a counter without any noise was
allowed to be a public foister; and he that could take
a piece of silver out of the purse without the noise of any
of the bells, he was adjudged a judicial nipper . . .*

Similar training, of course, took place in all periods under
Fagin-like tuition. Trained or not, all thieves found excellent
hunting grounds in the crowded markets, the big annual fairs,
and the visitors from the country and foreign parts who
thronged the narrow streets. In their turn, criminal and
vagabond elements attracted the attentions of authority who
retaliated with severe and merciless measures. The least that
authority could do was to keep vagrants on the move, as
proclaimed in 1593;

*An order is to be printed and set up in the City that all
poor, aged and impotent persons repair to the place
where they were born or where they were most con-
versant during the space of three years, there to be
maintained; likewise all others wandering about as
beggars, being whole and strong in body and able to
get work, having no lands or other means to get their
living shall be taken as rogues and vagabonds. And if
any impotent person so provided for wander abroad
out of his parish without licence he shall be whipped
and returned, but if eftsoons he offend again then to be
punished as a rogue.*

If authority operated continually against the thief and troublemaker, darkness was on their side. The streets really were dark.
After the sun had set, all shops would close and house lights
would be dimmed. The only other lights were the cressets
carried by the Mayor's officers and patrolling watch, who were
far from being efficient, and by individuals moving on foot or
on horseback. Naturally, the darkness concealed many forbidding dangers. This was the time when not only the rowdy
faction came out to harass travellers but also the moment when
ruffians and desperadoes would take over from the small time
thieves such as foists and cutpurses. There were orders right up

to the early eighteenth century that people should stay off the streets at a certain time and that public places should close after dark. In spite of this, there were always enough people about to become victims of frequent armed robbery or large-scale theft.

The first move to create general lighting was made in the early part of the fifteenth century when the Mayor ordered lanterns to be hung in the streets between the first of November and Candlemas. But in 1588, when every shadow could have concealed a Spaniard (this was the year of the Armada), all householders were ordered to hang lights outside their doors. At first, the penalty for disobeying was death, but then the penalty was reduced to one shilling and kept in force for over a century, when a public lighting company was formed. By 1685, a contractor called William Hemming had been retained to place a lamp outside every tenth house in the main streets between 6 p.m. and midnight, when they were extinguished. The lamps were usually glass globes with cotton wicks soaked in whale oil and hung either from gateways or poles fixed in walls or placed on posts. These globe lamps were maintained by lamplighters with ladders and were augmented by lanterns outside houses and shops.

Under the Westminster Paving and Lighting Act of 1762, a large proportion of the lighting was taken over by the Corporation but even then most of the side-streets were still unlit. The Watchmen still patrolled with their lanterns, crying the hour and thus warning thieves and footpads of their presence. Light could be hired by the individual in the form of a link-boy who walked in front carrying a torch of spluttering pitch and tow.

The Innocent are put in Terror, affronted and alarmed with Threats and Execrations, endangered with loaded Pistols, beat with Bludgeons and hacked with Cutlasses, of which the Loss of Health, of Limbs, and often of Life, is the Consequence; and all this without any Respect to Age, or Dignity, or Sex.

Henry Fielding, *An Enquiry into the Causes of the Late Increase of Robbers*, 1751.

Sometimes the link-boy was a member of a gang, and would lead his victim into a dark ambush. In 1810, the new gas-light was introduced and this immediately made the main streets safer. It took a long time, however, for poorer areas to receive gas and eventually electricity for lighting, and thieves were able to vanish quickly into murky corners and alley-ways.

If criminals were helped by darkness, so were they, too, by having their own areas to live in with considerable immunity from the authorities. Perhaps the most famous ruffians' centre was Southwark which has been mentioned as Alfred's southern bulwark to London. The settlement grew in size and eventually became a royal borough with a right to hold a fair and a market. An important factor in Southwark's growth was that at one time the gates of London which included London Bridge were closed at night. Travellers entering the City from the south were often benighted and so Southwark became a centre for inns. Alongside the inns, brothels flourished, and indeed the area held a royal licence for this purpose until Henry VIII cancelled it.

After the middle of the fourteenth century, the City of London made an effort to rid itself of gangsters, thieves and murderers. All that happened was that large sections of the underworld moved over the river to Southwark which now consolidated its position as a major haunt of criminals and whores. The City could not touch Southwark because it was outside the jurisdiction of the Mayor. The traffic, then, was two-way; citizens of London would cross over to sample the flesh-pots of Southwark which included bear-gardens, while the desperadoes of Southwark would cross the river the other way, sometimes by boat, to prey on the citizens. Eventually, the City obtained a foothold south of the river. Southwark was divided into three areas called liberties and one was owned by the monastery of Bermondsey and the prior of St. Mary Overy. After the Dissolution of the Monasteries, this liberty became royal property and was then, in 1550, sold to the City. The other two liberties, that of Paris Garden and that of the Clink, remained free of regulations and censorship and it was here that London's early theatres, so condemned by the authorities, were able to develop without harassment. It was fortunate for literary posterity that Shakespeare's plays could be presented in the Globe theatre with freedom from civic restriction.

Beggars as well as actors were glad to stay outside the City limits in Southwark. In 1595:

> There continue to be erected great numbers of poor tenements, which they call 'pennyrents', in Southwark and Kentish Street, wherein are placed a great company of very poor people. These having no trade nor honest endeavour to maintain themselves, not to pay their rent (which must usually be done at the week's end), make it their daily occupation to beg in the streets of the City.

However frustrating Southwark must have been to the Lord Mayor, sheriffs and marshalmen, the liberty which belonged to the City was very much subject to order, presumably as a buffer to dangerous disorders in the other two liberties.

Kentish, or Kent Street, is now Tabard Street. It linked the end of the Roman Watling Street with London Bridge and all travellers and pilgrims from Kent approached London along it. For centuries, Kent Street had a disreputable character as a haunt of the underworld particularly as a place where stolen goods could be disposed of. Smollet said of Kent Street in the eighteenth century:

> A foreigner, in passing through this beggarly and ruinous suburb, conceives such an idea of misery and meanness as all the wealth and magnificence of London and Westminster are afterwards unable to destroy.

Another street in Southwark with a similar malignant reputation to that of Kent Street was Bermondsey Street which was once described as 'pestilential'. Three other Southwark streets in the same area which harboured thieves, and lawbreakers for a long time were Lombard Street, Mint Square and Mint Street. Only a part of Mint Street remains today, as the whole area of ill-fame was cleared in 1877.

Back in Tudor times, the City itself had pockets in which criminals congregated and where no respectable person would live. The Barbican was one such spot but this area lost its evil reputation in the early seventeenth century because the Spanish Ambassador was living there in 1618. Another unsavoury district centred around Turnmill Street which lay outside the

walls to the east of the Fleet Ditch. Turnmill Street was infamous
well into Jacobean times, its image bolstered by many references
to it in Elizabethan drama. The area around St. Katherine by
the Tower was also a low haunt, frequented by sailors and their
companions. The fact that there were many breweries in this
part of London may well have contributed to its popularity.

Rogues and beggars made ample use of churches, too. After
the Reformation, the long nave of St. Paul's became a favourite
place for loungers and people seeking to do business. Apart
from providing shelter, St. Paul's was a shortcut which saved
a walk around the churchyard. In 1598, Bishop Bancroft was
told that St. Paul's was

> '.... *A common passage and thoroughfare for all kinds
> of Burden bearing people as Colliers with sacks of
> coal . . . also a daily recepticle for rogues and beggars
> however diseased, to the great offence of religious-
> minded people.*'

Another description tells how cony-catchers waited in the
nave for their victims, apprentices planned riots and how lovers
kept appointments with their mistresses. For respectable people
as well, St. Paul's was a convenient place to gossip, examine
posters, buy broadsheets and hire servants. Despite a proclamation, business agreements were made in the nave right up to the
time that St. Paul's was burned down in the Great Fire. The

My face I'll grime with filth;
Blanket my loins; elf all my hair in knots;
And with presented nakedness outface
The winds and persecution of the sky.
The country gives me proof and precedent
Of Bedlam beggars, who, with roaring voices
Strike in their numb'd and mortified bare arms
Pins, wooden pricks, nails, sprigs of rosemary.

Edgar in *King Lear* by Shakespeare.

authorities themselves, however, were not above using the big church for purposes other than worship. During the early fifteenth century, St. Paul's was the scene of many trials for heresy and witchcraft. Those found guilty were burned to death at neighbouring Smithfield. Roundhead troops were also quartered at one time in the nave.

In another respect, criminals before 1540 could use the facilities of churches to advantage. This was the right of claiming sanctuary. To remove anyone from a consecrated building or shrine amounted to sacrilege, although many fugitives from justice were starved out. In Britain, the murder of Becket in sanctuary in 1170 made the Church determined to enforce its own powers against secular authority. Westminster Abbey had considerable traditional rights in sanctuary matters. The poet Skelton fled there in 1527 after satirising Cardinal Wolsey and stayed until he died two years later. In 1540, an Act declared that offenders accused of murder, robbery and other felonies could not be protected by sanctuary. The same Act set up seven cities of refuge, including Westminster, where sanctuary limits remained in force. In practice, many places associated with religious foundations still retained rights of sanctuary, even after ecclesiastical sanctuary was abolished by statute in 1623. Almost naturally, debtors, wanted criminals, and fugitives from press gangs concentrated in these areas which became formidable centres of the underworld and dangerous for strangers to enter.

One such sanctuary, the precinct of St. Martin-le-Grand, which was linked to the Westminster sanctuary, was called 'the most troublesome thorn in the side of the City police' in Tudor times. Another well-known sanctuary was the Whitefriars quarter, known as Alsatia, which stretched from Salisbury Court to the Temple. While Whitefriars was primarily a debtors' stronghold, it sheltered undesirables of the worst kind. Macaulay describes Alsatia as it was in 1685:

> *Insolvents . . . were to be found in every dwelling, from cellar to garret. Of these, a large proportion were knaves and libertines, and were followed to their asylum by women more abandoned than themselves. The civil power was unable to keep order in a district swarming with such inhabitants. Though the immunities legally belonging to the place extended only to cases of debt,*

cheats, false witnesses, forgers and highwaymen found refuge there. For amidst a rabble so desperate no peace officer's life was in safety. At the cry of 'Rescue', bullies with swords and cudgels, and termagent hags with spits and broomsticks, poured forth by hundred; and the intruder was fortunate if he escaped back into Fleet Street, hustled, stripped and pumped on.

There were other places where offenders could find sanctuary. These included the Savoy in the Strand, Milford Lane (between Whitefriars and the Savoy), the Minories by the Tower, the Clink in Southwark, and Coldharbour, a district of small tenements in Dowgate Ward. While these refuges varied in size, they all followed the same progress from debtors' sanctuaries into iniquitous sinks. Finally, the City authorities had had enough. At the end of the seventeenth century, the sanctuaries were put down, and, in moves resembling the game of musical chairs, the inhabitants were forced to find other areas which the authorities would find difficult to raid.

But the sanctuaries were not the only locations to hold dens of criminals. In the same period, augmented by overcrowding, the 'settlements' of thieves began to grow alongside the sanctuaries. These were centred in streets and alleyways in districts such as Drury Lane, Smithfield, Wapping, Shoreditch, Whetstone Park and Westminster. The isolation of these areas was all the more pronounced because they were not only outside the city limits but also because the richer citizens of London were starting to move westward to build large houses in fashionable districts such as Holborn and Bloomsbury. There was another division between rich and poor in sixteenth century life, too. The City merchants tended to be puritanical in outlook and Parliament men closed the taverns, theatres and pleasure gardens with the exception of Bartholomew Fair. They also forbade sporting pursuits such as bull-baiting and cock-fighting which might attract large crowds. More than ever, London's dregs of people took up a warren-like existence, appearing from their grim holes in the slums to commit mischief and then slipping away out of sight.

There were names given at this time to the thieves who specialised in certain kinds of theft. For example, *Sneaking Budgers* took articles off stalls, *Prad-layers* cut saddle bags from horses, and *Dubbers* were thieves who picked locks. Handkerchief thieves were known as *Clouters*, and those who broke into houses with tools were known as *Mill-layers*.

Pepys records a robbery by one Colonel Turner, 'a mad, swearing, confident fellow, well known by all, and by me'. Turner had robbed an old merchant of money and jewels after gagging him in bed. More than twelve thousand people turned up a fortnight later to watch Turner's hanging. Turner was typical of a growing breed of criminals which was to terrorise high roads and streets around London with armed robbery for over a century—the highwaymen. These men were usually of high intelligence, or even of good family and education. Before Pepys's time, many of them would have turned to crime after losing money in the Civil War as Royalists. Later, this kind of criminal would start his career as a result of debts or loose living. The result was the same. The Common London thief was joined by a daring, dangerous rogue who took chances in robbing richer members of society. Travelling in the London area became more hazardous than ever.

One famous highwayman—or woman—who died a year after Cromwell was Mary Frith, or 'Moll Cutpurse' as she was known. Mary, ex-pickpocket and receiver of stolen goods, disguised herself as a man and is said to have been active in the profession in West London at the age of 60. She became so well known that a play was written about her—*The Roaring Girle* by Thomas Middleton and Thomas Dekker. Mary was also one of the first women to smoke tobacco, the habit which Sir Walter Raleigh had made popular. Very few highwaymen escaped the gallows but Mary was one of them. She was able to buy herself out of trouble with the money she had amassed.

Pepys saw the most distinguished highwayman of the sixteenth century hanged, the Frenchman Claude Duval. In fact, Pepys missed an important meeting with the Parliamentary Commissioners of Accounts to go to Tyburn. Duval was a footman who came to England when his master, a nobleman, returned here at the time of the Restoration after being in exile. Duval combined a reputation for charm with that of an accomplished card-sharp and con-man. He soon gave up his job as footman and became a professional criminal. At the age of 27, he was caught when dead drunk. It was reported that crowds of ladies visited Duval in Newgate and many more in masks witnessed

his execution. Others came to see his body lying in state at an
inn in St. Giles. An inscription on a stone in Covent Garden
church summed up his public image:

> *Here lies Du Vall: Reader, if male thou art,*
> *Look to thy purse; if female, to thy Heart . . .*
> *Old Tyburn's glory, England's illustrious thief,*
> *Du Vall, the ladies' Joy, Du Vall the ladies' grief.*

In 1682, was born the man who dominated crime in the early
eighteenth century. His name was Jonathan Wild who became
infamous as a thief-taker and one who specialised in the recovery
of stolen goods. Wild's contribution to London's criminal
history is that he was a 'Mr. Big', never actually committing
offences, but controlling the rogues who did so. In the age
before an adequate police system was established, conditions
were more than favourable for the activities that Wild master-
minded.

Wild was born in Wolverhampton in 1682, the eldest son of
a respectable carpenter. Jonathan, a short, lame man, served
his time as apprentice to a local buckle-maker and became a
journeyman. He was married and a father by 22. A year later,
he came to London as manservant to a lawyer, but returned to
his trade in Wolverhampton within a short time. However, the
call of the big city was too much for him and Wild left his wife
and child to work in London as a journeyman. Before long, he
fell into debt and was imprisoned in the Wood Street Compter,
a prison packed with felons and debtors. Here Wild learned
everything about crime and, more important, about its rewards.
The Compter gaolers allowed him to earn money by running
errands and, before long, Wild became underkeeper of prisoners
brought in on night charges. On his release, Wild became tenant
of an alehouse in Cripplegate and here he began his career,
based on the valuable contacts he had made in prison.

In 1691, legislation ruled that all buying or receiving with
knowledge that the goods were stolen made the receiver an
accessory after the fact. Thus both thief and receiver could be
hung on conviction. Wild saw that if he never was in possession,
he could never receive. So he set himself up as a broker between
thief and victim. He would gain details of thefts from his
acquaintances in the underworld and then inform the owners

of stolen goods where to go and what to pay to recover their goods. Wild took his commission from the thieves. Business boomed, and in 1717 Wild had an office conveniently near the Central Criminal Court, and a branch office.

He was clever enough to realise that if thieves were never brought to justice, then there would be tighter laws and precautions against offenders. Wild therefore became a thief-taker. This meant that he betrayed thieves for reward to the ministers of justice. By these means, Wild ensured that the villains who worked for him were kept under control. In fifteen years, Jonathan Wild informed against more than one hundred and twenty thieves. No wonder the underworld hated and feared him. There was a scale of rewards payable to informers. For instance, the conviction of a highwayman was worth £40, that of a horse-thief £10, while a deserter brought to justice was worth only £1. Wild added to his income by exporting stolen goods to Holland and smuggling by return cargoes of spirits.

But the Government had at last seen how Wild was benefiting no one but himself. In 1718, an Act initiated by Sir William Thompson was passed which laid down that people who took rewards for recovering stolen property and doing so without catching the thief were to be guilty of the same offence as the thief. The Act became known as the Jonathan Wild Act. In 1725, Wild was arrested for procuring the escape of a person accused of felony. But while he was lodged in Newgate, further charges were made accusing him of stealing lace and receiving a reward for recovering the lace without apprehending the thieves. Wild was convicted on the second charge and sentenced to death. The Judge was Sir William Thompson.

On a 'ticket' to Wild's execution was printed:

IONATHAN WILD THIEF-TAKER GENERAL
OF GREAT BRITAIN & IRELAND
To all Thieves, Whores, Pick-pockets, Family Fellons
& in Great Brittain & Ireland. Gentlemen & Ladies.
You are hereby desir'd to accompany yr worthy friend
ye Pious Mr. I - W-d from his Seat at Whittingtons
Colledge (e.g. Newgate Prison founded by Sir Richard
Whittington) to ye Tripple Tree, where he's to make
his last Exit on ———, and his Corps to be Carry'd from

> *thence to be decently Interr'd amongst his Ancestors.*
> *Pray bring this Ticket with you*

On the morning of his execution, Wild tried to poison himself by swallowing laudanum. But he took too much and vomited it up. In a dazed condition, he was conveyed to Tyburn where the Hangman decided to give him more time to recover. However, the huge crowd threatened the hangman with assault if Wild was not dealt with speedily. The hangman then acted quickly to carry out the sentence.

The hanging of Wild by no means finished off the profession of thief-taker. Indeed, thief-takers were an important part of the convention of how crime should be tackled at the time. The other belief was that crime should be paid for by severe punishments. All that happened was that thief-takers became richer (in 1787, £15,000 was paid out to informers) and that hangmen had more, rather than less work to do. At the end of the century, executions took place at the average of one a fortnight. All this was at a time which showed that London was one of the most lawless capitals in Europe. Armed robbery reached a peak with incidents taking place frequently both in central districts such as Holborn, Bloomsbury and Mayfair as well as in the suburbs and high roads leading to the City. William Lecky, the historian, wrote concerning this period:

> *William IV was accustomed to relate how his great-grandfather George II, when walking alone in Kensington Gardens, was robbed by a single highwayman who climbed over the wall, and pleading his great distress, and with a manner of much deference, deprived the King of his purse, his watch, and his buckles. Even in the most central parts of London, highway robberies were not infrequent. Thus, George IV, when Prince of Wales, and the Duke of York were robbed on Hay Hill near Berkeley Square. Two daughters of Admiral Holborn were driving across St. James's Square on their return from the Opera, when a single footpad stopped their carriage and carried off their watches and jewels. The Neapolitan Ambassador, though two footmen stood behind his carriage, was stopped in Grosvenor Square and robbed of his watch and money.*

Suburban roads were so dangerous that in 1746 the lessee of Marybone Gardens, a well-known place of entertainment, hired soldiers to protect patrons on their journeys to and from London. Later, a ten-guinea reward was offered for the capture of any highwaymen found on the road leading to the Gardens. Marybone Gardens was the scene of operations of the Highwayman Captain Macheath and his gang in *The Beggar's Opera*. Other dangerous districts included Blackheath, Richmond and Hounslow.

Highwaymen were as popular with the public as famous stage and screen personalities are today, particularly when they were being hanged. Then, they were expected by tradition to win the praise of the witnessing crowd by bold and carefree behaviour as befitted 'knights of the road'. The effect of hanging as a deterrent to a career of armed robbery was thus negated and there were still recruits to perpetuate the profession even though more than two hundred and fifty highwaymen were hanged between 1749 and 1771. In the footsteps of Mary Frith and Claude Duval came personalities such as James M'Lean, William Parsons, Paul Lewis and Jack Sheppard.

James M'Lean was the son of a Scottish Presbyterian minister and received a good education. His father left him a reasonable amount of money but he spent it all within a year. After working for two rich households, M'Lean tried unsuccessfully to start his own business as a grocer. When the business failed, he took to the road to earn money as a highwayman. Soon M'Lean had procured enough money to live in St. James's in lavish style with a mistress. During the day, his activities were law-abiding enough, but at night he pursued his career as a highwayman. Known as the 'Gentleman Highwayman', M'Lean was always polite to his victims. He was eventually caught selling stolen goods to a pawnbroker and was imprisoned in Newgate, where many members of society visited him, three thousand on a single day. M'Lean was twenty-six when he was hanged at Tyburn.

William Parsons was an Old Etonian and nephew of the Duchess of Northumberland. His criminal career began through incurring gambling debts. At one time, Parsons held commissions in the Army and Navy but he took to forging documents to gain credit for gambling. He was arrested and transported to Virginia where he escaped and became a successful highwayman. Returning from the colony to carry on with his new career in his native land, Parsons was caught on Hounslow Heath and suffered the usual capital fate at Tyburn.

Paul Lewis was another clergyman's son. Like Parsons, Lewis had been sent to a good school and had become an Army officer. His progress was typical of his profession; a downwards slide into gambling, drinking and whoring activities led to robbery on the highway to gain income. Boswell saw Lewis in Newgate before he was hanged:

> Paul . . . was a genteel, spirited young fellow. He was just a Macheath. He was dressed in a white coat and blue silk vest and silver, with his hair neatly queued and a silver-laced hat, smartly cocked. An acquaintance asked him how he was. He said, 'Very well'; quite resigned. Poor fellow! I really took a great concern for him, and wished to relieve him. He walked firmly and with a good air, with his chains rattling upon him, to the chapel.*

The next day, Boswell saw Lewis's execution: 'I was most terribly shocked, and thrown into a deep melancholy.' That night, Boswell could not sleep alone and went to stay with his friend the Hon. Andrew Erskine. If Boswell and other members of his class had shown less sympathy and more hatred to educated criminals, then the era of the highwayman would have been a great deal shorter.

The greatest celebrity of all highwaymen was undoubtedly Jack Sheppard. His fame, however, did not depend so much on his robberies (he stole no more than thirty shillings on the road) but on his spectacular escapes from prisons. Sheppard, described as 'pale, slight, boyish-looking', managed to find a way out of St. Giles's Roundhouse, the New Prison in Clerkenwell and the Condemned Hold, Newgate, from which he escaped twice. Articles, ballads, pamphlets, books were written about Sheppard and hundreds of visitors paid money to see him chained in Newgate. On the day of his execution in 1724, a huge crowd filled the streets between Newgate and Tyburn. The ensuing disturbances caused the Magistrates to read the Riot Act and send for a company of Guards. For over a hundred years afterwards, the public never tired of reading accounts of the

---

* *Boswell's London Journal*, edited F. A. Pottle (Heinemann)

adventures of Jack Sheppard.

The men who took the first positive action to prevent armed robbery rather than concentrating on the catching and conviction of criminals were Henry Fielding and his blind half-brother John. Henry had tried various careers by the time he became magistrate at Bow Street in 1748. He had been a barrister, theatrical producer, satirist and novelist. He became a magistrate in order to earn some money. Fielding's predecessor at Bow Street was Thomas de Veil, a man who had made strenuous efforts against London's criminals and could claim that he had sentenced or transported nearly two thousand major criminals. Fielding decided to maintain Bow Street's reputation in this achievement, and published his *Inquiry into the Causes of the Late Increase of Robbers* in 1751. Putting his ideas into practice, Fielding first organised a group of six, efficient parish constables based on Bow Street ('Mr. Fielding's People') and launched a public relations campaign using notices in the press to keep the public informed of their existence and success of this little force. The constables were the forerunners of the Bow Street Runners. By this time Henry had been joined by John and, at the request of the Government, the two brothers prepared a plan for dealing with armed robbery and murder. The plan was relatively simple. The Fielding brothers suggested that, given the required funds, the Bow Street office should remain open with a magistrate on duty for twenty-four hours a day. Also on duty should be two runners with horses, able to set out anywhere immediately and who should be paid whether successful or not. Other proposals were the setting up of a register of all crimes, criminals and suspects, and the establishment of a fund to reward anyone supplying the office with information concerning criminals. Again, the Fieldings recommended that maximum publicity should be given to the new Bow Street Runners and to wanted criminals and stolen property. After procrastinating for some time, the government approved the Fieldings' plan and it was put into operation. Almost immediately, good results were obtained and by early 1753, the year when Henry Fielding died, violent crimes, pickpocketing and housebreaking were obviously on the decrease.

Many highwaymen, though, were still escaping. John Fielding suggested that residents on the outskirts of London should form clubs to provide messengers to ride swiftly to Bow Street after a crime had been committed. From this idea came the famous Horse Patrol of ex-constables, soldiers and others who numbered ten in 1763. The men in the Horse Patrol were stationed at the turnpike gates (everyone leaving or entering London had to do so by these gates; hence Turnpike Lane) to be ready to pursue any highwaymen. The Horse Patrol was successful from the start; so successful that the Government disbanded it during the next year. The highwaymen returned to plague the roads shortly afterwards, and the Patrol was reassembled for a few months. Once more, the highwaymen were dispersed. But this time, on the grounds of cost, the authorities refused to grant sufficient funds to allow the Patrol to continue, and within ten years the incidence of armed robbery was great as it had ever been.

Not until 1805, was the Government persuaded that the Horse Patrol was essential in controlling the crimes committed by highwaymen. This time, the Patrol was allowed to remain in existence, and the days of highway robbery began to fade into the past. In this respect, London began to lose a little of its evil reputation and crime was forced to become more subtle as the police grew more efficient.

If the underworld had its heroes in Regency London, it had nothing remotely glamorous to show in Victorian London. The conditions which bred crime were at their worst. In 1841, one person in eleven was a pauper and the unemployment rate was ten per cent. The movement of classes within London had produced hideous slums for the working classes which absentee landlords left to ferment and produce profit. For London's submerged poor, as Bernard Ash puts it, 'the nineteenth century held in store horrors enough to have made even a medieval rabble flinch'. It was the old story of over-crowding again, but this time the inhabitants were surrounded by built-up areas and had to contain themselves within their sordid surroundings. Several of these concentrations concealed dangerous criminals and the worst places were known as rookeries.

As has been explained, after the rich classes move out from a town to the suburbs, the poor are left in areas that ring the original town, particularly its original part. Naturally, the buildings where the poor congregated were never improved. What did happen was that owners of property for profit's sake filled every available space, including gardens, with new buildings. From this policy came the warrens in which members of the underworld hid. In Victorian times strangers entered these mazes at their own peril, as they did the sanctuaries of the seventeenth century, and many of the rookeries developed in quarters which had been traditional centres of criminal activity. Many of the worst criminal slums also were situated near to districts where spoils could be gained—districts where the affluent lived or where there were entertainments such as theatres or saloons.

There were some parts of London which had especially large collections of disreputable slums which in term shielded every kind of squalor and savagery. In general terms, these quarters were across the Thames centred on Southwark; in the East End embracing districts such as Whitechapel; behind Westminster Abbey; in the region of Clerkenwell; and in the neighbourhood of St. Giles.

South of the river, criminals lay low in Lambeth and Bermondsey as well as the Old Mint and Old Kent Road. The East End slums and dens were in districts with well-known names such as Spitalfields, Stepney, Bethnal Green, Petticoat Lane, and Ratcliff Highway. At Westminster, there was the Devil's Acre near Westminster Abbey and warrens full of disease near St. James's; Clerkenwell had the well-known Saffron Hill which Dickens toured. And St. Giles with the nearby Seven Dials and Drury Lane became the most infamous thieves' citadel of all.

What did all these slum pockets have in common? All of them were overcrowded to extremes. In some districts as many as thirty people of all ages might live in one room, probably with no furniture apart from ragged bedding and straw. In St. Giles, it was estimated that three thousand people lived in less than a hundred homes. The resulting sanitary conditions in these 'netherskens' were indescribable and for most of the century sewage and water supply were hopelessly inadequate. A feature of many slums were the netherskens, or low lodging houses, of all sizes. Kellow Chesney describes the tenants in the context of all Victorian cities (*The Victorian Underworld* by Kellow Chesney, Temple Press):

> *Here were to be found specimens of all the types of the social sump. A big rookery nethersken might harbour a shifting collection of casual labourers,*

hawkers, beggars, thieves, low night-stand prostitutes, petty touts and sharpers, road sweepers, street performers, broken servants and more or less unspecifiable riff-raff. Nevertheless, as with most places where people gather together, there was a tendency for those who shared the same interests to favour particular houses. Some were literally thieves' kitchens, chiefly frequented by pickpockets, house robbers and their confederates, while others were largely tenanted by beggars. Others again enjoyed a special reputation as 'servants' lurks' where out of work servants of bad character congregated, often ready to make plans for robbing their employers.

In his famous work *London Labour and the London Poor*, Henry Mayhew devoted several pages to netherskens, of which he estimated there were at least 200 in London. One 'reverend informant' told Mayhew of the licentiousness of many inmates of these boarding houses, particularly where 'the sexes are herded together indiscriminately':

Boys have boastfully carried on loud conversations, and from distant parts of the room, of their triumphs over the virtue of girls, and girls have laughed at and encouraged the recital. Three, four, five, six, and even more boys and girls have been packed, head and feet, into one small bed; some of them perhaps never met before. On such occasions any clothing seems often enough to be regarded as merely an incumbrance. Sometimes there are loud quarrels and revilings from the jealousy of boys and girls, and more especially of girls whose 'chaps' have deserted or been inveigled from them. At others, there is an amicable interchange of partners, and next day a resumption of their former companionship . . . Even in some houses considered of the better sort, men and women, husbands and wives, old and young, strangers and acquaintances, sleep in the same apartment, and if they choose, in the same bed. Any remonstrance at some act of gross depravity, or impropriety on the part of a woman not so utterly hardened as the others, is met with abuse and derision.

It was realised by mid-century, that reform of the netherskens was far overdue. The first move for bringing them under control came with the Common Lodging House Act of 1851 which introduced measures such as regular police inspection, the registering of inmates and the setting of basic standards of decency. Fines and the threat of closure in breach of the act resulted in the disappearance of the worst lodging houses and the dispersal of their inhabitants. Much of the atmosphere of the London rookeries was captured in the engravings by Gustave Doré published in the 1870's.

One of Doré's illustrations depicts a fracas in the Ratcliffe Highway, the slum area regarded as the most dangerous and toughest. Today, the street is known just as 'The Highway', and its present surroundings in dockland are far removed from its sordid past. The links with the sea provided the Ratcliffe Highway with representatives of every nationality which sailed the seas. De Quincey, who described murders there in his essay *Murder considered as one of the fine arts*, wrote:

> . . . *Manifold ruffianism shrouded impenetrably under the mixed hats and turbans of men whose past was untraceable to any European eye.*

Fights, murders, sailors' brothels, stolen nautical goods; all could be found in the dark lanes and alleys surrounding this horrific area. Scuffles resulting in death or injury were liable to break out at any time and any visitor to the area of possible affluence was lucky if he escaped being attacked.

The arch-rookery of all was, of course, St. Giles. Its notoriety lasted from the seventeenth century to the middle of the nineteenth. The 'Holy Land', as St. Giles was called, lay in the area bordered by the British Museum and St. Giles Church. Compared to other London rookeries, St. Giles was not outstanding either in danger or size (it covered some eight acres) but it became the best situated centre from which the underworld operated. As in advertisements for houses, the Holy Land was 'in easy reach of the West End'. Thieves and beggars had only short distances to travel to enter districts where there were rich pickings. What was just as important for men on the run was that once inside the rookery, they were as safe as if they had entered a fortress. The Holy Land was a maze of passageways,

A tavern door fracas on the Ratcliffe Highway engraved by Doré. *RADIO TIMES HULTON PICTURE LIBRARY*

tunnels and hideouts, linked by escape routes, covered and littered with filth. It was a brave policeman who ventured to chase a criminal into the dark, twisting labyrinths.

Mayhew's colleague John Binny, who contributed to *London Labour and the London Poor*, quotes from a report by a Mr. Hunt, inspector of police, who tells of one such brave police officer:

> *I remember on one occasion, in 1844, a notorious thief was wanted by a well-known criminal officer (Restieaux). He was known to associate with some cadgers who used a house in the rear of Paddy Corvan's, near Church Street, and was believed to be in the house when Restieaux and a serjeant entered it. They went into the kitchen where seven male and five female thieves were seated, along with several cadgers of the most cunning class. One of them made a signal, indicating that some one had escaped by the back door of the premises, in which direction the officers pro- ceeded. It was evident the thief had gone over a low wall into an adjoining yard. The pursuers climbed over, passed through the yard and back premises of eleven houses, and secured him in Jones Court. There were about twenty persons present at the time of the arrest, but they offered no resistance to the constables. It would have been a different matter had he been apprehended by strangers.*

In the same report, Mr. Hunt describes other premises in the same area of the Holy Land:

> *The houses in Jones Court were connected by roof, yard, and cellar with those in Bainbridge and Bucker- idge streets, and with each other in such a manner that the apprehension of an inmate or refugee in one of them was almost a task of impossibility to a stranger, and difficult to those well acquainted with the interior of the dwellings. In one of the cellars was a large cesspool, covered in such a way that a stranger would likely step into it. In the same cellar was a hole about two feet square, leading to the next cellar, and thence by a*

*similar hole into the cellar of a house in Scott's Court,
Buckeridge Street. These afforded a ready means of
escape to a thief, but effectually stopped the pursuers,
who would be put to the risk of creeping on his hands
and knees through a hole two feet square in a dark
cellar in St. Giles's Rookery, entirely in the power of
dangerous characters. Other houses were connected in
a similar manner . . .*

The St. Giles's rookery flourished until 1847. In that year, a
new street was driven straight through the middle of the Holy
Land. This new way was named New Oxford Street and by
destroying many of the squalid lairs of the rookery, forced the
inmates to disperse to other districts. Charles Dickens made a
tour of one of the remaining slums of the Holy Land, Rats'
Castle, in 1850. Rats' Castle was 'within call of St. Giles's
church'.

John Binny, too, visited thieves' dens in Spitalfields, 'one of
the most notorious rookeries for infamous characters in the
metropolis'. Needless to say, he was accompanied by a policeman. One of the haunts they visited was a public-house with
a 'ruffian-looking' landlord:

*We found two or three brutal-looking men loafing about
the bar. We passed through a small yard behind the
house, where we found a number of fighting dogs
chained to their kennels. We went to another outhouse
beyond, where between thirty and forty persons were
assembled round a wooden enclosure looking on, while
some of their dogs were killing rats. They consisted of
burglars, pickpockets, and the associates of thieves.
Many of them had the rough stamp of the criminal on
their countenances . . . This is one of the most dangerous
thieves' dens we have seen in London. Were any unfortunate man to be inveigled into it in the evening, or
at midnight, when the desperadoes who haunt it are
inflamed with strong drink, he would be completely in
their power, even were he the bravest soldier in the
British service, and armed with a revolver.*

South of the St. Giles's rookery was another evil centre, Seven Dials, called after the seven-sided cross-roads which still exists today. Criminal tradesmen of this district went in for marketing counterfeit currency. There were also several presses which turned out street-ballads and 'confessions' of criminals destined for the Newgate gallows. Some gangs in Seven Dials used large guard dogs to warn and protect them, should any unwelcome strangers approach their hiding places. The population of this thieves' warren received a large boost when the Holy Land began to be broken up. In its turn, Seven Dials was brought under control as the efficiency of the police improved.

Three other rookeries are worthy of mention; the Hoxton area centred on Whitecross Street and Golden Lane, the district between Bishopsgate and Aldgate around Petticoat Lane, and the Lisson Grove area of Marylebone. As would be supposed, rookeries on the fringes of the city swelled when the central ones were reduced. But even they were eventually subdued. Then, like the surrender of a besieged city, the chief rookeries were taken over by social reformers, city planners and the law.

In many respects, Victorian criminals resembled their Elizabethan counterparts. There was the equivalent of the counterfeit crank, the beggar who faked injuries. There were shoplifters, footpads and card sharps. As in Elizabethan times, each type of thief had its own slang name. For instance, *skinners* were thieves who stole clothes off children. *Dragsmen* (this sounds like twentieth century slang) stole luggage off carriages. A *gonoph* was a common street thief, inferior to members of the swell mob. Readers familiar with *Oliver Twist* will know that the 'kinchin lay' was the pursuit of stealing errand money from children.

There were burglars of all varieties, too. Some were chimney sweeps who were usually experienced climbers. Others were servants in big houses in league with a gang. At the time of the American Civil War, London suffered a series of street robberies in which the victims were seized by the neck, either with a piece of material or by an arm. This method of robbery was known as garotting.

John Binny, in his contribution to Mayhew's *London Labour and the London Poor*, mentioned that other robberies in this period were 'perpetrated by brutal violence with a life-preserver or bludgeon'. These were usually committed by women with support from male partners. In Binny's example:

> *The woman walks forward, or loiters about, followed by the men, who are hanging in the rear . . . She picks up a man in the street, possibly the worse for liquor; she enters into conversation, and decoys him to some quiet secluded place, and may there allow him to take liberties with her person, but not to have carnal connection. Meantime, she robs him of his watch, money, or other property, and at once makes off.*

Should the victim pursue the woman, her 'bodyguard' steps in and stops him.

> *In some cases a quarrel arises, and the victim is not only plundered of his money, but severely injured by a life-preserver or bludgeon.*

In Binny's view, the attic or garret thieves were 'generally the most expert thieves in the metropolis'. These jewel thieves entered houses through attic rooms, having made their way along gutters and coping. They would take care to choose a time when the family—and the servants—were engaged with dinner. Binny reported a 'very remarkable robbery' of this kind in 1861 at Lowndes Square, where the thieves stole jewellery worth £3,000.

The numbers and influence of these petty criminals was directly linked with the poverty and misery of the working classes. Only when society in the shape of social reformers, efficient policemen and a sympathetic public acted together did the swarms of small-time thieves reduce. At last some of the profits of Empire could be turned to tearing down slums, educating the poor and providing employment that would help to make crime a less necessary way of earning a living. The Victorians also made respectability fashionable and this characteristic became essential in the climb up through the intricate class structure.

But the twentieth century brought new problems engendered by militant minority groups or by changing social attitudes. After the Fenians came, as we have seen, Anarchists, Nihilists and then Suffragettes. Before the First World War ended there was an increase in the White Slave Traffic. After the War, moral standards dropped and the crime rate rose as a result. Drug trafficking began to be a serious problem. The Second World War brought the several espionage and spying cases, centred around the Russian Embassy in London. Names of agents such as Fuchs, Blake, Vassall and the Krogers became well known. There was a tendency for criminals to operate in gangs to attempt armed robberies or bullion ambushes.

Some modern gangs cause more terror today in London than any gang of Victorian footpads lurking near a rookery. One such gang was that led by the twin Kray brothers who were sentenced to life imprisonment for murder in 1969. The gang terrorised the East End for many years, so intimidating its neighbourhood that no one dared reveal its activities in corruption, protection rackets and murder. The police investigations were described as 'most painstaking and often courageous'. At the end of a 40-day trial at the Central Criminal Court, Ronald Kray was found guilty of the murder of two men. Reginald was found guilty of one of the murders and of being an accessory after the fact to the other. The twins' elder brother Charles was also convicted of being an accessory after the fact to one murder and was sentenced to 10 years. In dismissing the Krays' appeals, the Court of Appeal said that:

> . . . *each murder was committed in cold blood and without obvious motive; each bore the stamp of a gang leader asserting his authority by killing in the presence of witnesses whose silence could be assured by that authority.*

However extensive modern gang activities may be, they hardly infringe on the life of the average citizen. Gone are the days when a walk at night in London's streets laid the pedestrian open to fierce and brutal assault by robbers for the smallest gain. There are certain times which can be perilous, of course. A visit to the casualty department of any large London hospital after the pubs have closed on Saturday night reveals people who have been involved in the same kind of incidents as their ancestors were through the centuries.

CHAPTER SIX

CRUEL MURDER

> K. Richard. *But didst thou see them dead?*
> Tyr. *I did, my lord.*
> K. Rich. *And buried, gentle Tyrrel?*
> Tyr. *The chaplain of the Tower hath buried them;*
> *But where, to say the truth, I do not know.*

IN SHAKESPEARE'S *Richard III*, the king asks Sir James Tyrrell, his Master of the Horse, for confirmation of the murder of his two young nephews. The boys were sons of Edward IV who died in 1483. The elder boy, who was 12, was thus Edward V, and the younger, aged 9, was Richard Duke of York. However, their ambitious uncle, Richard Duke of Gloucester, had usurped the throne as Richard III and had imprisoned the boys in the Tower of London on the death of their father.

Later that year, Richard decided to eliminate the boys as claimants to the throne. The Keeper of the Tower, Sir Robert Brackenbury, refused to carry out the order and Richard had to approach Tyrrell with the assignment. Tyrrell had no scruples and found two men to carry out the foul deed. The men were Green, Tyrrell's groom, and Forest, one of the jailers in charge of the princes. Green and Forest smothered the boys with pillows, after which, according to Edward Hall's *Chronicles*, they

> . . . *layd the bodies out upon the bed, and fetched James Tirrel to see them, which when he saw them perfightly dead, he caused the murtherers to burye them at the*

*stayre foote, metely deepe in the ground under a great
heape of stones.*

This account is at variance with Shakespeare's except that
both agree that the bodies were buried in the Tower. When two
skeletons of boys were found near the Wakefield Tower nearly
two hundred years later, their remains were reburied in Westminster Abbey in the belief that they were the princes.

To list all the premeditated killings that have occurred in
London would take several volumes, especially as London in
this respect was a city where violent death was almost a daily
happening. There are, though, several murders in London's
history which always arouse interest and some of them have
been selected for inclusion in this chapter.

The murder of the princes had been preceded by another
abhorrent killing in the Tower five years previously. The
princes' uncle, George, Duke of Clarence, had been found
guilty of treason. There were three charges against him. First,
Clarence was accused of having a horoscope cast to find out
when his brother, King Edward IV, would die. Then he started
a rumour that the king was not entitled to the throne because
he was illegitimate. The third charge was that Clarence had
taken steps to rebel against his brother. A court under the
Duke of Buckingham heard the charges and condemned him
to death. The details of Clarence's death are uncertain, but the
story goes that after his murder, his body was pushed into a
water butt which had once held malmsey. The folk version is
that Clarence was drowned in the wine.

One famous London murder which took place a century later
is also associated with drink. The well-known poet and dramatist
Christophere Marlowe was killed one summer night in 1593 at
the Bull Inn, Deptford. Marlowe, who was suspected of being
'an atheist, a blasphemer, given to the vice of sodomy', had
spent the afternoon at the inn with three friends. The men had
dined and walked in the garden until evening, when they had
returned to the inn for supper and no doubt for further drinking.
Marlowe quarrelled with one of his friends, Ingram Frizer,
about the bill. Suddenly, Marlowe sprang up from the bed on
which he had been lying, and attacked Frizer who was sitting
at the table. Marlowe took Frizer's dagger from his back and
wounded him twice in the head. Frizer to save his life tried to

94 EVIL LONDON

retrieve his dagger, and in doing so, stabbed Marlowe over the right eye which killed him immediately. The Coroner found that Frizer had acted in self-defence.

The year before, a man and a woman were executed at Smithfield for murder by poison of the woman's husband. The couple in this Bywaters-and-Thompson kind of murder (Bywaters murdered his lover's husband in 1922) were Anne Brewen and John Parker. Anne Welles, as she then was, was admired by two young goldsmiths, John Brewen and John Parker. Brewen gave her gold and jewels as part of his efforts to win her favour, but she refused his hand, having become Parker's lover. Brewen then demanded his gifts back. Anne refused, and to her shock, Brewen had her arrested for theft. She was so astonished that she promised, if Brewen dropped his charge, that she would marry him. He was delighted but Parker, of course, was not. He began to taunt Anne and before long she regretted having made such a promise. Within three days of her marriage to Brewen, she made plans to poison him. She had refused to live with her husband until he had found a better house and had found lodgings not far from Parker's home so that she could meet him conveniently.

Parker now brought her some poison which she mixed in a pudding and gave to her husband. Within twenty-four hours, he was dead. None of the neighbours became suspicious until two years later, Anne and Parker were heard quarrelling. Parker had refused to marry her and she was pregnant by him. Some neighbours reported the revelations of the quarrel to the magistrates and the two were arrested. They both denied the murder, but Anne was told separately that Parker had confessed to it. She then revealed everything. Both were condemned after her child was born. Anne was burnt alive after Parker was hanged before her eyes.

Not long after, another celebrated poison case occurred, this time in higher circles. Robert Carr, Viscount Rochester, had paid court to Frances Howard, the young Countess of Essex, with the help of Sir Thomas Overbury. When Overbury learned that Carr, the royal favourite, intended to marry the Countess if she could get a divorce, he tried to prevent Carr from taking such a step. Carr realised that Overbury might ruin the divorce proceedings so he persuaded the king to have Overbury placed in the Tower. Here Overbury was doomed, because Carr and

Frances Howard began to poison him slowly by arranging that his food contained poison. The Lieutenant of the Tower, Sir Jervis Elwes, was aware of this action, and condoned it.

Overbury became very ill. After a month, he realised what Carr was up to and wrote to Carr that he had set down all the details of the events and that the document was going to be sent to friends who would circulate it. No such document was ever found but as a result of Overbury's letter, Frances Howard and an accomplice, a Mrs. Anne Turner, bribed an apothecary's assistant to administer sublimate of mercury to Sir Thomas. The unfortunate man died forthwith in agony and was buried in the Tower. The divorce and subsequently the marriage of Carr and Frances Howard went through. Carr now became the Earl of Somerset.

Two years later in 1615, retribution struck. The apothecary's assistant fell ill and confessed to his part in the murder. The law went into action. Before long, Mrs. Turner, Sir Jervis Elwes (who had been removed from his post), another accomplice and the doctor who had provided the poisons were all hanged. At her execution Mrs. Turner wore starched yellow ruffs; these now became unfashionable for many years. Carr and Frances Howard were sentenced to be beheaded. On four occasions, crowds gathered at Tower Hill to see the execution. But in the end, the king pardoned the couple who were then imprisoned in the Tower for five years and afterwards banished to their house at Greys.

In the year after the Great Plague, Pepys writes about a murder:

> 9th May. *In our street, at the Three Tuns Tavern, I find a great hubbub: and what was it but two brothers had fallen out, and one killed the other? And who should they be but the two Fieldings? one whereof, Bazill, was page to my Lady Sandwich; and he hath killed the other, himself being very drunk, and so is sent to Newgate.*
> 10th May. *At noon to Kent's at the Three Tuns Tavern: and there the constable of the parish did show us the picklocks and dice that were found in the dead man's pocket, and but 18d. in money; and a table-book, wherein were entered the names of several places where*

he was to go; and among others his house, where he
was to dine, and did dine yesterday. And after dinner
went into the church, and there saw his corpse with the
wound in his left breast; a sad spectacle, and a broad
wound, which makes my hand now shake to write of it.
His brother intending, it seems, to kill the coachman,
who did not please him, this fellow stepped in and took
away his sword; who thereupon took out his knife,
which was of the fashion, with a falchion blade, and a
little cross at the hilt like a dagger; and with that
stabbed him.

More London murders must have been committed near taverns than in any other location, and this murder borders on the commonplace. But a murder which has been mentioned already and which took place some dozen years after the Fielding one has been called one of the great mysteries of crime. The murder was that of Sir Edmundbury Godfrey, the London magistrate. In October 1678, Sir Edmundbury's corpse was found in a ditch near Primrose Hill. He had been missing for five days. Someone had attempted to make the death look like suicide because Sir Edmundbury's sword was placed in his body as if he had fallen on it deliberately. However, it was obvious that the wound had been inflicted after death.

In the public's mind, there was no doubt that the murderers were Roman Catholics. This was the time when there was a strong anti-Catholic feeling in London whipped up by people such as Titus Oates who had been alleging the existence of a Papist Plot to take over the country. Indeed, Oates had visited Godfrey a fortnight before with information about alleged Roman Catholic plotters which the magistrate was investigating. Praunce, a Catholic working at Somerset House, the residence of the Queen, was arrested with some others and had confessed, implicating five men. Three were caught—Robert Green, Henry Berry, and Lawrence Hill—and stood trial for the murder. The trial has been described as a travesty of justice. Praunce's 'confession' was contradicted in two capital respects. The three men, who attempted to prove that they were nowhere near Primrose Hill on the night in question, were hanged, all protesting their innocence to the last. Lord Birkenhead wrote after studying the trial:

. . . An impartial observer is left with the uncomfortable feeling that Oates and his colleagues, or unscrupulous men behind them, may perhaps have committed the murder in order to rouse popular feeling against the Catholics. Whether that be so or not, can never be settled. The murder of Sir Edmundbury Godfrey must remain an insoluble mystery.

Another trial of legal interest took place in 1693 when Charles, Baron Mohun of Okehampton, was tried by his fellow peers at Westminster Hall for the murder of Will Mountford, actor. The man who actually committed the murder was one Captain Hill, who had fled. Mohun had assisted Hill in an attempt to kidnap an attractive actress called Bracegirdle. Hill had made advances to Mrs. Bracegirdle but was rejected because, Hill believed, she was the mistress of Mountford. Mohun and Hill attempted to force the lady into a carriage but failed to do so. Help came and Mrs. Bracegirdle was able to go home. The two would-be kidnappers paced up and down outside with drawn swords. A message was sent to warn Mountford about Hill, but Mountford did not receive it and by chance met the two men. The Captain ran his sword through Mountford who died the next day. In the absence of Hill, Mohun went on trial but was acquitted, probably because Hill had acted without premeditation. Mohun was just 17.

Seven years later, Mohun again stood before his peers on a charge of murder. This time, Mohun, the Earl of Warwick and a Captain Coote had a drunken dispute with three other revellers at the Greyhound tavern in the Strand when they were waiting for sedan chairs late one evening. The six men proceeded to the area of Leicester Square and after a confusing fight in the dark, Coote was found dead, run through twice with a sword. Mohun had a slight wound on his hand and was arrested. He claimed that he had gone to the fight only after failing to stop the others from going on with the murderous fight. The Lords unanimously found Mohun not guilty.

In 1729 came some murder charges which at the time were regarded as sensational. Two Wardens of the Fleet Prison and the Deputy Warden of the Marshalsea Prison were accused separately of murdering prisoners in their respective prisons after an investigation by a Select Committee of the House of

Commons. The causes of death of the prisoners concerned were in the main brought about by the damp, filthy condition of these debtors' prisons, and the prosecution could not prove intent to murder in any of the six trials. All the prison officials were thus acquitted.

In one trial, Thomas Acton, Deputy Warden of the Marshalsea, was charged with murdering John Bromfield, an Army captain. Bromfield was in prison for debt and had in some way annoyed Acton, because he was beaten, placed in irons and put in a hole under the stairs. Here, the wretched man could not stand upright or lie at full length. According to one witness, this cell was about as big as a large coffin. The floor was just bare earth and too damp to lie on. After several days in this hole, Bromfield fell ill and died—just over three months after entering the prison. Acton claimed that Bromfield was put in irons because he stabbed another prisoner and that he was well when released, but then caught jaundice which killed him. The jury, as in other cases, believed the defendant. However, the publicity given to the trials affected some improvements to these dark, unventilated gaols, even though public sympathy tended to be on the side of the Wardens, rather than the prisoners who had died.

In 1726, Mrs. Catherine Hayes murdered her husband by battering in his skull. But she did not stop at that. With the help of two friends, she dismembered his body and distributed the portions in various parts of London. Mrs. Hayes was condemned to be strangled and then burnt. Unfortunately, the fire at Tyburn was lit before the executioner placed the rope around her neck. The flames scorched his hand and he was forced to let go of the rope, leaving her to be roasted alive.

Seven years later, another murderess held the town aghast. She was Sarah Malcolm who killed her mistress and two fellow servants. Sarah strangled two of her victims and cut the throat of the third. She became notorious. Many people believed she was innocent and regarded her as a heroine. Hogarth painted her portrait after a visit to her cell. However, according to one comment:

> It seems strange that she found anyone to look upon
> her as a heroine, for although only twenty-five years
> old, the bloom of youth had vanished, and she was a

*sombre creature with harsh and forbidding features.**

Sarah Malcolm was hanged in Fleet Street between Mitre Court and Fetter Lane, 'her cheeks painted in honour of the occasion', as close to the scene of her infamy as possible and in the presence of a vast crowd of spectators.

A murder which made people realise that no one was immune to violent death happened in 1812, when Spencer Percival, the Prime Minister, was assassinated. The murderer was a madman called John Bellingham, who shot Spencer Percival in the lobby of the House of Commons. Percival was the only Prime Minister to be murdered and has a monument in Westminster Abbey showing him falling after being shot. Bellingham was tried and convicted three days after the murder, and was executed three days after the trial.

Towards the end of the eighteenth century, a demand grew for human bodies that was to become a dilemma for medical students and a means for making money by criminals with ghoulish inclinations.

Previously, judges would add to the sentence of a criminal condemned to be hanged for a particularly brutal crime that his body should be handed over to surgeons and students for dissection. But in the early part of the nineteenth century, there was a large increase in the number of medical students and the supply of bodies was not enough to satisfy the demand. A new profession arose, that of Resurrection Man. In its simplest form, this was merely selling unclaimed bodies to medical schools. But this trade developed into an occupation even more horrible; that of marking down fresh graves, exhuming the contents and selling the corpses to anatomists before decay set in.

Two gentlemen in Edinburgh took the process even further. William Burke and William Hare found that it was more profitable and easier to obtain bodies by murdering people without marking them too violently. Burke and Hare were able to sell some sixteen bodies to the Medical School in Edinburgh at prices ranging from £6 to £10. Burking, as the business came to be known, was controlled by the Anatomy Act of 1832 which regulated the supply of bodies to medical schools.

---

* Horace Bleackley, *The Hangmen of England* (1929).

In London, Burke and Hare were emulated by John Bishop and Thomas Williams. These burkers killed their victims near Friar's Mount, Bethnal Green, and invoked this comment from William Cobbett in *Two-Penny Trash* not long before the Anatomy Act was passed:

> *The College of Surgeons allow, that even they are not, in all cases, able to distinguish between* murdered bodies and bodies stolen from the coffin. *The cutter-up and the receiver* never know *that they* are not accessories *to the commission of murder, they proceed in their bloody work, knowing that they may be such accessories. No man, nothing short of a monster, will deny that it is* as great *a crime to steal the dead body of a human being, as it is to steal the dead body of a pig or sheep. Therefore, that crime ought to be punished* with death *as is the crime of stealing the dead body of a pig or sheep; and* death *ought also to be the punishment of the* receiver *and the* cutter-up.

Bishop and Williams were hanged at Newgate in 1831 for the murder of Charles Ferrair, a little Italian boy. From the moment the two men appeared on the scaffold, the vast crowd hooted and hissed at them. Such was the pressure of the mob that all the numerous crowd barriers in the Old Bailey gave way. There were many accidents; for example, more than twenty people were seriously maimed and taken to hospital before half past seven in the morning.

Popular opinion, together with the law, ended the macabre profession of burking. But from now on, an increasing audience of newspaper and journal readers were able to read about murders almost as they happened. In 1840, a seventy-two-year-old peer, Lord William Russell, was murdered at his house in Norfolk Street, Park Lane, by his Swiss valet François Courvoisier. This murder made a considerable stir. Courvoisier, who had cut his employer's throat, said that he had been inspired to do so by a stage production of the adventures of Jack Sheppard. The Lord Chamberlain then banned plays with 'Jack Sheppard' in their title. Courvoisier was hanged outside Newgate. Two writers were in the watching crowd of 20,000; Dickens and Thackeray, who stood for four hours outside the prison.

Dickens attended another execution a few years later, that of Mr. George and Mrs. Marie Manning on the top of Horsemonger Lane Prison. The couple were sentenced for murdering Patrick O'Connor, her lover, in Bermondsey and burying him under their kitchen floor. Confessed Mr. Manning (who had condoned his wife's affair): 'I never liked him well, and I battered his head with a ripping chisel.' With Dickens was John Leech, the artist, who had been commissioned by *Punch* to illustrate the scene. Mrs. Manning, a Belgian described as 'passionate' and 'handsome and robust, a hard relentless siren destitute of morals', wore black satin for the event, and as with the yellow ruffs of Mrs. Anne Turner two centuries previously, the material went out of fashion. In his letter to *The Times* written immediately afterwards, Dickens said:

> *I do not believe that any community can prosper where such a scene of horror as was enacted this morning outside Horsemonger Lane Gaol is permitted at the very doors of good citizens and is passed by unknown or forgotten.*

Another murder which caused a buzz of interest was one committed in 1875 by a one-time lecturer at the London Institutes. Henry Wainwright was hanged at Newgate (executions were now behind closed doors) for murdering a mistress called Harriet Lane. After the murder, Wainwright, 'one of the most zealous churchmen of his neighbourhood', dismembered the body and wrapped the mutilated members in two parcels which were found in his possession. He was hanged three months later. The Sheriffs allowed nearly 100 spectators to watch the execution, after which children were seen playing a game called 'Wainwright'. In the game, the trial and hanging were enacted, and in one case a fatal accident nearly occurred to the boy playing the role of Wainwright.

Wainwright was executed by the hangman William Marwood. Four years later, Marwood was to hang Kate Webster at Wandsworth prison, a 'savage and malicious' Irishwoman who had dismembered her mistress and thrown the pieces into the Thames. Another well-known client of Marwood's was the

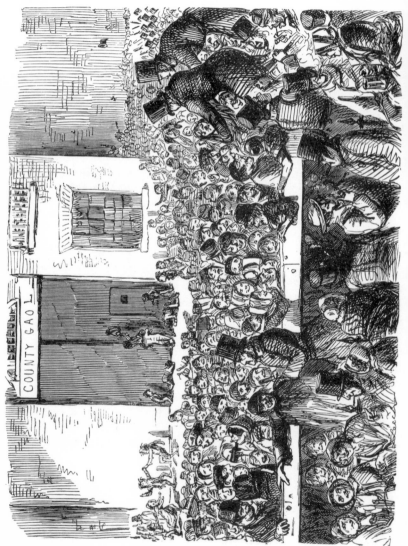

'The Great Moral Lesson at Horsemonger Lane Gaol, Nov. 13' was Leech's caustic caption to his Punch cartoon of the crowd at the hanging of Mr. and Mrs. Manning in 1849.

poisoner Dr. George Lamson, who administered aconitine to his brother-in-law who was at school at Wimbledon. Lamson was executed in 1882.

London at this time had developed an effective detective force at Scotland Yard. This force had come into being after a brutal and shocking murder at Roehampton. Between 1839 and 1842, London had no equivalent of the Bow Street Runners, as no more appointments were made. But in 1842, the blood-thirsty murder of Mrs. Good demonstrated that a regular detective force would be an asset in capturing criminals.

An East Indian merchant living at Roehampton employed a coachman called Daniel Good, who lived at the stables which were situated a mile from the main house. In April, Good bought a pair of black knee breeches on credit at a local pawn-broker's, but was seen shoplifting another pair of trousers. The pawnbroker accused Good of the theft, but Good denied the charge and drove off in his master's chaise.

A constable was sent to arrest Good, and was guided to the stables by a boy who knew where Good lived. Good admitted the theft and offered to pay for the trousers. On instructions, the constable then tried to search the stables but Good refused

---

Beneath this stone
are deposited the remains of
Ellen Lefevre
Aged 23 years
and her four children
Henry aged 5 years and 6 months
John aged 4 years and 6 months
Ellen aged 2 years and 6 months
Philip aged 8 months
who were murdered at their residence in Southampton Street Pentonville during the night of Monday 8th September 1834 by Johann Nicholas Steinberg aged 45 years a native of Germany and father of the above children who afterwards murdered himself and was buried according to law.

Tombstone at St. James's, Clerkenwell.

to let him in. However, the bailiff of the estate appeared and gave the constable permission to enter the stables. Good showed reluctance and again offered to pay for the trousers. The constable continued to search the stalls, looking under the hay piled there. To his horror, he found the headless and limbless body of a woman.

Good then rushed out of the stable, locking the door on the constable, bailiff and boy. When the door was forced open, Good had disappeared. While a doctor was examining the body, an obnoxious smell was sensed coming from the harness room. In there, the macabre head and limbs of the woman were found in the fireplace, where someone had tried to burn them. A blood-stained axe and saw were also discovered.

Public apprehension increased considerably when the police admitted that they had found no trace of Good. There was considerable alarm at the fact that a violent criminal was loose in the London area and that the authorities had no efficient means of finding him. Eventually Good was caught in Tonbridge, convicted and hanged. He had murdered Mrs. Good because he had fallen in love with another woman who had been pressing him to marry her.

In order to deal with any similar situation involving a wanted murderer, the authorities established a small section of eight detectives attached to Scotland Yard to cover the London area. This was the beginning of this famous police establishment.

Alarmed as the public had been over having Daniel Good at large, their panic was nothing like that engendered in the East End by the depraved Jack the Ripper murders of 1888. In the ten-week period between August 31st and November 9th, five women were seized from behind and had their throats slit. All the murders took place within an area about one-quarter mile square in the dark alleys and corners of the Whitechapel area. All but one of the bodies were mutilated in some way, and in two of the murders organs were removed from the bodies. All five victims were killed either on the first weekend of the month or the last, between 12.00 and 5.00 a.m. After the fifth murder, Queen Victoria sent a telegram to the Prime Minister, Lord Salisbury:

> *This new most ghastly murder shows the absolute necessity for some very decided action. All these courts*

must be lit, and our detectives improved. They are not what they should be. You promised when the first murder took place to consult with your colleagues about it.

But the Cabinet did not have to revolutionise Scotland Yard. The murders ceased abruptly after that. The murderer was never found, even though various suspects have been discussed ever since. These have included a barrister and a member of the Royal Family.

The victim killed on August 31st was Mary Ann Nicholls, a 42-year-old prostitute. She was found lying in the gutter in Bucks Row, now Durward Street. Mary Ann, or Polly as she was called, had had her throat cut almost from ear to ear together with deep wounds in her abdomen which almost disembowelled her. The Ripper's second victim was found on September 8th in Hanbury Street with the same wounds in her throat and abdomen as Polly Nichols had, but with even more mutilation. She was Annie Chapman, 47, also a prostitute.

Both these ghastly murders aroused fear in the East End and endless speculation in the Press. A further period of terror and sensation was to follow at the end of the month when Jack the Ripper struck twice in the night of September 30th. Elizabeth ('Long Liz') Stride, 45 and of Swedish origin, had her throat cut in the courtyard under the windows of the International Workmen's Educational Club, Berner Street, where members were singing. Long Liz was seen alive at 11.45 p.m. and it was one o'clock when a hawker drove his horse and cart into the

---

A lodger named Davis was going down to work and found the woman lying on her back close to the flight of steps leading into the yard. Her throat was cut in a fearful manner. The woman's body had been completely ripped open, and the heart and other organs laying about the place, and portions of the entrails round the victim's neck.

From a broadsheet at the time of the Jack the Ripper murders in Spitalfields, 1888.

yard outside the club and discovered the still-warm body. It appeared that the horse and cart, clopping along, had frightened the killer away.

But the Ripper had plenty of time to deal with his other victim that night. Catherine Eddowes, 43, had been in custody for drunkenness at Bishopsgate police station less than an hour before she was found murdered in Mitre Square. A policeman had passed through the square at 1.30 a.m. and it was empty. Twenty minutes later, passing through the square again, he discovered the dead, mutilated body of Eddowes. She had had her throat hacked, face gashed, part of her right ear cut off, and her intestines pulled out and draped over her right shoulder. Half an hour later, a bloodstained piece of the victim's apron was found five streets away. The Acting Police Commissioner for the City of London, Major Henry Smith, found bloodstained water in a public sink in Dorset Street where the Ripper had paused to wash his hands.

The Ripper's worst and most abhorrent mutilations were carried out on his last and youngest victim, Mary Kelly, on the night of November 9th. Mary, 24, also a prostitute, was heard singing in her room at Miller's Court, Dorset Street (now Duval Street) at 1 a.m. Just before 11.00 a.m. the same morning, she was found dead, horribly mutilated. Jack the Ripper had burnt some clothes in order to see as he worked, and it was considered miraculous that no inhabitant of Miller's Court had noticed the fire or seen the Ripper at a job which must have taken him two hours, according to estimates. He had cut the features off his victim's face as well as slicing her throat in his usual manner. He had then proceeded to open her abdomen and remove most of her organs which were laid out beside her body.

The previous concern over the Ripper's murders was nothing compared to the distress and alarm which arose after his fifth terrible murder. But before long, Scotland Yard withdrew its extra detectives from the East End, and life returned to normal in Whitechapel. It was generally believed by authority that Jack the Ripper had committed suicide. Whoever he was, the Ripper was someone who not only had some surgical knowledge but also had an extensive knowledge of the geography of the East End. The Ripper was also able to win the confidence of his female victims.

In books written in 1965* and 1972† respectively, two writers, Tom Cullen and Daniel Farson, contend that Jack the Ripper was Montague John Druitt, a barrister turned teacher, who committed suicide by throwing himself into the Thames in December, 1888.

If the police would not or could not name the Ripper, they had an outstanding success a few years later when they solved the Muswell Hill murder. An old man called Smith was found bound with his head battered in. Inspector Lambert of the Yard found two sets of footprints in the garden. The original burglar alarm set up by the old man which involved a loaded shotgun had been dismantled by someone who must have made a previous reconnaissance. Inside the house, the Inspector found a safe broken open and a small bulls-eye lantern. When the list of paroled convicts was checked, two men were found who had not reported to the police. Their names were Milsom and Fowler. When Inspector Lambert visited Milsom's mother-in-law, her young son recognised the lantern as his. The search was now on for Milsom and Fowler, who were found in Bath. Both were found guilty of the Muswell Hill murder and hanged.

In the following year, 1896, a celebrated baby farmer was convicted. She was Mrs. Dyer who strangled 46 of the babies she was paid to adopt and threw them in the Thames. Baby-farming thrived at this time because there were strong pressures, social and economic, on Victorian unmarried mothers to get rid of their children. They could do this by finding a woman prepared to take and adopt children in return for maintenance payments or a lump sum. When children in the care of baby-farmers died, it was very difficult to prove neglect or deliberate murder if there were grounds for suspicion. Of course, many mothers of illegitimate children, especially pro-stitutes, did not want to see their children again and this encouraged many evil abuses. In 1870 when another infamous baby-farmer, Mrs. Waters, was convicted of murdering an infant by poison and neglect, a conservative estimate of children in the care of baby-farmers was 30,000. The inhumanity shown to young children began to be checked by organisations such

* *Autumn of Terror*, **Jack the Ripper: His Crimes and Times (Bodley Head).**
† *Jack the Ripper* **(Michael Joseph).**

as the National Society for the Prevention of Cruelty to Children which was founded in 1884.

The first murderers to be convicted on fingerprint evidence were the Stratton brothers who killed an old shopkeeper and his wife in Deptford in 1905. A fingerprint on a rifled cash-box tallied with a print taken from Alfred Stratton who was seen with his brother in the neighbourhood earlier on. While the judge stated that the similarity between the prints was corroborative evidence to a certain extent only, the jury decided that the Strattons were guilty of the crime.

A poisoner whose victims were his three wives in bigamous marriages was George Chapman, alias Severin Klosowski, a Polish barber-surgeon. Chapman came to England a year before the Ripper murders at the age of 22. Indeed, several officials believed that Chapman was Jack the Ripper because he had certain surgical skills and because he was in London at the time of the murders. Chapman poisoned his first 'wife' with antimony in 1897 and four years later dealt with Bessie Taylor, a barmaid at the Prince of Wales, Finsbury, whom he had 'married' in the same way. Chapman's third bigamous wife died in the same way through 'exhaustion from vomiting and diarrhoea'. As this had happened in the year after Bessie's death and because Chapman had used strychnine to finish his victim off, his crime was discovered. He was arrested in October 1902, and subsequently condemned to death and hanged.

The great criminal sensation of 1910 was the trial of Dr. Crippen who had poisoned his wife with hyoscine, dissected her and buried her under the cellar floor of his house in Hilldrop Crescent, off Camden Road. He was also the first criminal fugitive to be captured with the aid of the new-fangled (as it was then) wireless telegraphy. Crippen's wife has been described as 'a woman of a flamboyant type, loud in her tastes and extravagant in her personal expenditure, but a parsimonious and slovenly housekeeper'. She had ambitions of becoming a music hall artiste, too.

When Crippen was nearly fifty, he fell in love with a girl who was the opposite in temperament to his wife; Ethel Le Neve, a typist at the medical firm where he worked. Early in 1910, Crippen announced that his wife had gone to America. Shortly afterwards, he published the news of her death. Not long after

The waxen Dr. Crippen in Madame Tussaud's Chamber of Horrors.
PICTURE BY JOHN GARNER, COURTESY OF MADAME TUSSAUD'S

that, he took Ethel to a dance where some of his wife's friends noticed she was wearing some jewellery belonging to Mrs. Crippen. Ethel then became the Doctor's housekeeper. Mrs. Crippen's friends became suspicious and the police began to make inquiries. An inspector called at the Crippen home to interview Ethel. Nothing would have probably been suspected if the inspector had not returned to Crippen's office three days later to make a trifling inquiry. Crippen had flown. His house was deserted. After searching it for two days, the police found the remains of Mrs. Crippen.

Crippen had taken Ethel, disguised as a boy, on board the S.S. *Montrose* which sailed on the 20th July for Quebec. The *Montrose* was fitted with wireless which the captain used to contact the police once he had recognised the wanted pair. The couple were arrested on the other side of the Atlantic by police officers who had overtaken them in a faster ship. In separate trials, Crippen was found guilty of murder but Ethel was acquitted of being an accessory to murder after the fact. Lord Birkenhead, the barrister who defended Ethel, wrote this of

Crippen's trial:

> *The trial had many noteworthy features which did not concern me, as they were not in any way part of my defence of Le Neve. The case will be for a long time the leading authority on the rule that a jury trying a charge of murder must not separate, for a juryman who felt ill was taken by the jurykeeper into the courtyard for fresh air and then returned to his fellows. It was held that there had been no separation of the jury to invalidate the trial. The scientific evidence both as to the detection of hyoscine and the identification of the body by a small mark on a tiny piece of skin aroused great interest and controversy. The medico-legal aspect of the evidence is of the greatest importance to all experts and lawyers who may be concerned in similar cases in future.*

Dr. Crippen was hanged and Ethel Le Neve went off to a new life in America.

Two years later, Londoners had another remarkable case to gossip about when a miser murdered a miser. Miss Eliza Barrow, 49, had capital of £4,000 plus a cash-box that she kept with gold and banknotes. She, her six-year-old adopted son Ernie, and two relatives, a Mr. and Mrs. Hook, became tenants of four rooms in a house owned and lived in by Frederick Henry Seddon in Tollington Park, North London. Seddon, a sales manager with an insurance company, was as preoccupied with money as Miss Barrow was. Soon he became Miss Barrow's confidant, and ejected the Hooks when she quarrelled with them. He offered her an annuity of £10 per month plus rent-free accommodation in exchange for her capital of stock and titles to a public house and an adjoining barber shop. Miss Barrow accepted, and insisted on her payments in gold.

Eight months later, Miss Barrow started to feel ill, with symptoms of vomiting and diarrhoea. The local doctors prescribed medicines but a month later, she was dead. When some of her relatives discovered that Seddon had acquired nearly all her property, they went to the police. The subsequent exhumation of Miss Barrow's body revealed arsenic in the tissues. Six months after Miss Barrow's death, Mr. and Mrs. Seddon went on trial for the murder of the dead woman. Mrs. Seddon was acquitted but Seddon was found guilty and hanged. The evidence was largely circumstantial, but Seddon could not explain how the arsenic had entered Miss Barrow's body while she lodged in his house. He also failed to explain many of his actions, for instance why so many banknotes belonging to Miss Barrow had been found in the possession of him and his wife. The Seddon trial has been declared as unique in the history of crime.

The executioner of Crippen and Seddon was John Ellis who in his career hanged nearly two hundred people. One of Ellis's last hangings was that of Mrs. Edith Thompson, executed in 1923 with Frederick Bywaters for the murder of her husband. Ellis was so overcome by the terrible scenes at Mrs. Thompson's execution at Holloway (she 'had disintegrated as a human being on her way to the gallows') that he tried to commit suicide. Ellis was quoted as saying that he was haunted by the ghost of Mrs. Thompson. He was successful in taking his life at a later attempt.

Ellis was not the only person affected by the hanging of Mrs. Thompson. Every official concerned, men and women, resigned; the prison chaplain became seriously ill; and a wardress present at the event became mentally unhinged. Mrs. Thompson was aged 28.

In 1928, Scotland Yard demonstrated its efficiency in modern police detection with the arrest of Frederick Guy Browne and William Henry Kennedy for the murder of Police Constable George Gutteridge who was found shot by the side of a road. The constable had been killed by two shots fired at his head at close range. Two further shots were fired at him as he lay on the ground, one at each eye. The brutality of the murder had 'shocked the country'. The investigations, involving forensic science and a long series of interviews, took several months. The only clues were two bullets found at the scene.

A curious parallel to the Jack the Ripper murders took place between January 1964 and January 1965. The murderer concerned became known as Jack the Stripper and like his famous predecessor was alleged to have committed suicide before he could be arrested. Jack the Stripper killed six prostitutes, all aged between 20 and 30. All of them operated in West London. None was taller than five feet two inches. All were stripped of their clothing. Each body was found within a few miles of the centre of London.

Hannah Tailford was found on the Thames foreshore near Hammersmith Bridge in February. Two months later, Irene Lockwood was found three hundred yards upstream from where Hannah had been found. The next nude victim was found in the same month in Brentford, not far from the scenes of the previous murders. She was Helen Bartholemy. The police became convinced that the murderer was a man who made casual pickups. Then in July a fourth victim was found, Mary Fleming, in a Chiswick cul-de-sac. By now, laboratory work had shown that the bodies of the last two victims bore dust particles with paint on them. From this clue, it was deduced that the bodies had been close to a place where cars were sprayed.

The police were still investigating Mary Fleming's death when Margaret McGowan was found in November in a car park at Hornton Street, Kensington. Finally, nearly a year after Hannah Tailford was found, Jack the Stripper's last victim was discovered in Shepherd's Bush. Bridie O'Hara also bore the same dust and paint particles carried by Irene and Helen. At one time, the murder force totalled five hundred policemen and policewomen. Policewomen were dressed up as prostitutes to trap the murderer, but no one took the bait.

Finally, paint spray premises were found in Acton which fitted the forensic evidence. Seven thousand people on the nearby factory estate were questioned. The suspects narrowed down to three, but the final suspect took his own life. As in 1888 like Jack the Ripper, Jack the Stripper killed no more.

There are many other names mentioned when murder in London is talked about. Neville Heath, the lady-killer; Haigh, the acid-bath murderer; Miles Gifford, who bludgeoned his parents to death; Bentley who was hanged for the murder of a policeman by his friend Craig; Christie, who killed his wife and at least five women; Ruth Ellis, who shot her lover and was the last woman to be hanged; Roberts, Duddy and Witney, who between them killed three policemen in thirty seconds: these are some of the names. The gunman, the knifer and the strangler still appear from time to time; the poisoner, however, seems to have retired. Murder, in any case, is no longer the chief cause of violent death in London.

The motor car has taken over.

CHAPTER SEVEN

PRISONS AND GAOLS

Of late the liberty of access unto such persons as are not close prisoners in the Tower hath been abused insomuch that some repair thither at undue seasons and sometimes stay after the gates be shut. Hereafter none shall be permitted to stay with any prisoner in the Tower either in his chamber or in any retired place there at the time of dinner, or supper, or divine services unless it be in the presence of the Governor. Nor shall any other than a preacher, physician, apothecary or chirurgeon be permitted to repair to the prisoners save between the hours of 8 and 11 of the clock in the forenoon, and between 1 and 4 of the clock in the afternoon.

THIS PROCLAMATION was posted up in 1599 after the authorities were concerned with the abuse by the public of visiting periods in London's premier prison, the Royal Fortress and Palace of the Tower of London. If you were imprisoned for committing crime in London, you were sent to the prison which matched your offence. The Tower was emphatically a political prison and fulfilled this solemn role up to the Second World War when several German spies and the Nazi leader Rudolf Hess were held there.

The modern role of the Tower is that of a museum, but in its time it has been a fortress, royal palace, armoury, mint and, until 1835, a zoo. Compared to the common prisons, the Tower was luxurious. The Countess of Somerset during her imprisonment there was allowed to install her own bedroom furniture (covered in red velvet), chairs, silver plate and various hangings. However, the pendulum of comfort occasionally swung the other way. In 1278, some six hundred Jews were prisoners in the sub-crypt below St. John's Chapel in the White Tower, having been blamed for clipping unmilled coinage. Conditions in the comparatively small, dark space must have been foul beyond description.

The White Tower, the large central keep, was built in 1078 possibly on the site of a Roman fort. Excavations have shown a portion of the Roman Wall and one of its bastions at the east of the White Tower. The purpose of the Norman fortress was dual; to protect and overawe the City. William I's architect was Gundulph, Bishop of Rochester, who had created a similar building in Rochester Castle. As a palace and place of residence the Tower was extended by Henry III. At this time, the keep was whitewashed, giving the building its name. The inner wall with its thirteen towers together with the moat was constructed during the reign of Richard I. Edward I completed the work of Henry III by strengthening or rebuilding the outer walls of the Tower. Rounded bastions were added to the wall on the north side by Henry VIII.

Among the distinguished prisoners in the Tower, four were foreign kings. In 1296, King John Baliol of Scotland was imprisoned after the battle of Dunbar. A second Scots King, David Bruce, was held in the Tower after the battle of Neville's Cross in 1346, and a third, James I of Scotland, spent two years there in 1406. King John II of France ('The Good') was also a prisoner for two years in 1358. For many people, a stay in the Tower was followed by a short walk to the scaffold. This happened to such figures as Sir Thomas More, Anne Boleyn, two Earls of Essex, Lady Jane Grey, the Earl of Strafford and Archbishop Laud. English history of the sixteenth and seventeenth centuries is full of their misfortunes. Later prisoners who escaped death included Pepys, John Churchill the future Duke of Marlborough, Robert Walpole, John Wilkes, Lord George Gordon and Roger Casement.

The Tower had not only an exclusive set of prisoners but also a unique collection of instruments of torture which were used on unfortunate victims such as the Gunpowder plotters. For example, a prisoner qualifying for torture would probably spend some time in the 'Little Ease', a hole under the White

Tower resembling that in the Marshalsea Prison. The Little Ease was found behind a small door with an iron grating at the top. It was just 18 inches wide, four feet high and two feet deep. A prisoner in the Little Ease would have his head forced down on his chest and would be unable to sit or lean in this private hell.

Another torture used by Tower gaolers was the 'gauntlets'. These were iron gloves suspended from a high beam in which the prisoner's hands were held up in the air by thumbscrews. At the same time, the victim had to stand on three wooden blocks. A refusal to confess would mean that one of the blocks would be knocked away with a mallet. The pain on the hands would be excruciating, especially as the sufferer would have to stand on tip-toe to support the weight of his body. If he refused to reveal the required information again, the next block would be struck away, causing agonising pain. The prisoner would now be hanging by his hands, remaining there until he lost consciousness, or until his torturers thought fit.

One sufferer described his feelings as follows:

> *I felt the chief pain in my breast, belly, arms and hands. I thought that all the blood in my body had run into my arms, and began to burst out of my finger ends. This was a mistake: but the arms swelled, till the gauntlets were buried within the flesh. After being thus suspended an hour, I fainted: and when I came to myself, I found the executioners supporting me in their arms: they replaced the pieces of wood under my feet, but as soon as I was recovered, removed them again. Thus I continued hanging for the space of five hours, during which I fainted eight or nine times.*

A famous instrument of torture which was invented by the English was the rack. This had an oblong shaped framework raised above the floor. The victim's legs would be tied to a fixed bar at one end, while his hands were fastened to a revolving bar at the other end. This revolving bar was turned by levers and pulleys to stretch the prisoner's body. A particularly stubborn victim could have his joints torn almost from their sockets. The rack was in use until 1728.

There were other means of making Tower prisoners talk.

One was a heated stone on which the sufferer was forced to sit until he confessed. Another way was to leave him in a flooded cell to the mercies of famished rats.

Prisoners were sent to this cell by special warrant of the Privy Council for the purpose of extorting confession. The terror of this dungeon came with the rise of the tide which covered the floor with stinking water. With the water appeared hordes of hungry and savage rats. A prisoner who slept risked hideous injury or death. He had to fight the rats in the water and in the dark. If he refused to confess, he would become weary and exhausted, an easy victim for the sharp teeth of the rats.

A diabolical piece of equipment used with great success in the Tower was the Scavenger's Daughter. This description comes from *The History of Torture throughout the Ages* by G. R. Scott (Luxor Press):

> *The Scavenger's Daughter was strongly made of iron hoops, consisting of two parts hinged together. The prisoner was forced into a kneeling posture on the floor, and told to draw his body and limbs together so as to compress himself into the smallest possible space. The executioner, having passed one of the iron hoops under the prisoner's legs, knelt upon his shoulders, forcing his body downwards until it was possible to fasten the two hoops together over the small of the back. The agony which the victim of this torture suffered must have been beyond all endurance, and there is little room for wonder that in most cases a confession was obtained before the expiration of the time (one and a half hours) allotted for confinement in the apparatus. It is stated that long before this the blood was spurting from the nostrils, the mouth, and the anus, and even, on occasion, from the hands and feet.*

Visitors to the Tower today can see a collection of implements used for torture in the White Tower.

If the Tower was the prison for the élite, grey, grim Newgate was the gaol for all common criminals in the City. All the western gates to the City, Newgate, Ludgate and Cripplegate, became prisons. The chambers on top of Newgate were a prison from the twelfth century on. The prison proper was built with money set aside under the will of Sir Richard Whittington, thrice Lord Mayor, who died in 1423. The same money built an alms-house called Whittington College and later many wits referred to the prison by this name. The new prison was built on the site of the older gate-house, which,

> 'because it was feeble, over little, and so contagious of air that it caused the death of many men, was thrown down'.

In its time, the gate-house was the subject of an inquiry which confirmed that the gaolers were extortioners who placed offenders for petty crime in with dangerous criminals unless they paid up. The gate-house was also a target of Wat Tyler's men in 1831, when it was wrecked. The building was, of course, destroyed in the Great Fire of 1666 and rebuilt. Newgate became notorious during the eighteenth century. At this time, the prison consisted of the old city gate that spanned Newgate Street, together with two annexes, four floors tall, joining it on either side of the roadway. All three sinister buildings were connected on each floor by staircases and passageways. The Condemned Hold was a dark, dismal dungeon on the ground floor in the southern annex; it measured twenty feet by fourteen. A heavy door with an opening protected by spikes on top of it led into the main entrance hall of the gaol. This, and a small barred window, gave the prisoners their only source of light. Visitors could talk with the prisoners through the opening on the door. In 1728, fifteen new cells were opened in place of the Condemned Hold. They were no improvement. Each was nine feet high, but measured nine feet by seven and were lighted by a tiny double-grated window. The result was that the cells were in semi-darkness. During the day, convicts were allowed to meet in a large room called the day-room where their friends could visit them, but at night the prisoners were locked up again in their cells. 'Prisoners shed tears upon being brought to these dark-some solitary abodes,' declared John Howard the philanthropist fifty years later. These condemned cells were still in use when Victoria came to the throne. Hundreds of visitors paid three shillings and sixpence each in 1724 to enter the Condemned Hold to stare at the manacled Jack Sheppard. Many of the visitors brought handkerchiefs, not to cry into, but soaked in vinegar to counteract the foul stench. An informative, but exaggerative, publication concerning Newgate first appeared in 1771—*The Newgate Calendar* or *Malefactor's Bloody Register*:

> '*containing Genuine and Circumstantial Narrative of the lives and transactions, various exploits and Dying Speeches of the Most Notorious Criminals of both sexes . . .*'

The grim building which had housed famous criminals such as Sheppard, Jonathan Wild, Captain Kidd and James M'Lean was burnt out again during the Gordon Riots of 1780 when 300 felons were released by the mob. The new Newgate which was a feature of Victorian London (it was designed by George Dance the Younger) was completed in 1783 and ceased to be a debtors' prison after 1815.

Lord George Gordon, instigator of the 1780 Riots, spent more than ten years in the new prison before he died there from gaol fever. Lord George was able to lead a life of comfort during this time. He threw parties in his cell and asked friends to dine with him regularly. Two servants looked after him, and newspapers and books were made available to him.

Before it was reformed, nineteenth century Newgate retained characteristics left over from the previous centuries: bribery and corruption among the prison officers, all prisoners (except those condemned to death) mixed together, and no adequate food or clothing for prisoners without money. In mid-century, Gustave Doré illustrated the shuffling line of despondent prisoners taking exercise in a Newgate exercise yard (there was one yard exclusively for the condemned).

Any infringement of the rule of silence was punished with flogging. Prisoners who were punished in this way were placed in a kind of pillory which held the hands, the lower part being a box which enclosed the lower part of the body. Another macabre custom was noted by Dickens when he visited Newgate Chapel in 1837. Prisoners condemned to death had to sit in the condemned pew on the Sunday before their execution in front of their fellow prisoners and join in the responses of their own burial service. Previously, the condemned men had to undergo the whole chapel service with their coffins beside them in the pew. The young pickpockets whom Dickens saw in Newgate

Above: The horrors of Bedlam as seen through Hogarth's eyes in 'The Rake's Progress'. Below: Doré's engraving of the Exercise Yard, Newgate. *BOTH ILLUSTRATIONS RADIO TIMES HULTON PICTURE LIBRARY*

gave him material for *Oliver Twist*. After the passing of the Prisons Bill in 1877, the prison became gradually disused. Newgate Prison was finally pulled down in 1902 and some of its stones were used in the construction of the Central Criminal Court—the Old Bailey—which now stands on the site.

One institution which confined wretched prisoners of another kind in London is still in existence, though now in West Wickham, Kent. This is the hospital of St. Mary of Bethlehem for the insane, which was known for centuries by the contraction of its name as Bedlam. The hospital was originally part of the Priory of St. Mary of Bethlehem founded in 1274 and situated near Moorfields. In 1403, the hospital had become an asylum with six lunatics and three sick persons there as inmates. In 1546, the Priory was dissolved as were other large religious houses and the hospital was handed over to the City and eventually placed under the control of the governors of Bridewell Prison. The hospital was situated between two open sewers and in the opinion of a visitor in 1598:

> *It was so loathsomely and filthily kept that it was not fit for any man to come into . . .*

The conditions in Bedlam may have been one of the reasons why a large crowd of 'prentices and divers others' rescued a silkweaver a few years before from being committed to the hospital as a madman by the Lord Mayor. The silkweaver had criticised the achievements of the Lord Mayor 'using some hard speeches'. Unwisely, the Lord Mayor had sent the culprit along to Bedlam escorted only by his servants instead of by officials. The procession was easy game for the apprentices.

Inside the hospital, the patients wandered about the buildings and yards. The more 'disturbed' inmates were chained up on beds of straw, and alternatively beaten or humoured. Bedlam gained revenue by allowing sightseers in, on payment of an entrance fee, to look around the hospital.

In 1647, a huge new hospital was completed at London Wall and until 1770 it continued to be one of London's great side-shows. Hogarth's *The Rake's Progress* included Bedlam in one of the sequences. At this time, admittance to see the lunatics was twopence. One popular patient was a man in a straw cap who promised he would declare war on the stars if he was given a bottle of wine. Strawcap also told visitors that he could summon hosts of eagles.

Visiting Bedlam to laugh at the inmates was a fashionable pastime among the rich until 1770, when the authorities decided that sightseers could make the patients even more mentally afflicted. In 1815, the hospital went to Lambeth, to the building where the Imperial War Museum is now. William Cowper wrote in 1784 of his visit to Bedlam when he was a boy:

> *Though a boy, I was not altogether insensible to the misery of the poor captives, nor destitute of feeling for them. But the madness of some of them has such a humourous air, and displayed itself in so many whimsical freaks, that it was impossible not to be entertained at the same time that I was angry with myself for being so.*

Another popular entertainment was provided by the infamous house of correction, Bridewell, where erring girls and women, usually prostitutes, were whipped in front of members of the court of governors and spectators. In 1677, a balustrated gallery was erected for the public to use during the whippings. The practice continued for almost another century.

Bridewell, near the malodorous Fleet Ditch, was once a Norman fortified palace. Then Henry VIII rebuilt it, but in 1553 Bridewell was handed over to the City to become a house of correction and a workhouse for the poor. It became a model for similar institutions all over the country. In the London area, Westminster and Surrey Bridewells became well known as local houses of correction. The inmates of the City Bridewell were usually vagrants and 'troublesome whores' but in Elizabeth's reign religious nonconformists and captured Spanish sailors were imprisoned there, as well.

In the seventeenth century, Bridewell became a common gaol for criminals arrested in its neighbourhood. Terms of imprisonment in Bridewell were usually short—from seven days to two years—and the prisoners were kept busy picking oakum and beating hemp. Pepys tells us how he was involved with men who were caught by the press gang in 1666 and placed in Bridewell without money or food.

Mightily troubled all this morning with going to my Lord Mayor, (Sir Thomas Bludworth, a silly man I think,) about getting shipped some men that they have these last two nights pressed in the City out of houses: the persons wholly unfit for sea, and many of them people of very good fashion, which is a shame to think of, and carried to Bridewell they are, yet without being impressed with money legally as they ought to be. But to see how the King's business is done; my Lord Mayor did scruple at this time of extremity to do this thing, because he had not money to pay the pressed-money to the men. I did out of my own purse disburse £15 to pay for their pressing and diet last night . . .

The prison and its chapel were finally pulled down during 1863–71.

Westminster Bridewell, in Tothill Fields near Horseferry Road, began in 1633 as an institution for the employment of indolent paupers. Like the senior Bridewell, it became a house of correction, and finally a criminal prison. It lasted until 1885. Not far away at the Abbey End of Tothill Street stood the Gatehouse Prison, built by Edward III and pulled down in 1776. Perhaps its most famous prisoner was Sir Walter Raleigh who spent the night before his execution there in 1618. A former page to the household of Charles I, Sir Jeffery Hudson, was imprisoned in the Gatehouse in 1679. Hudson was a twenty-inch-tall dwarf who was once served up to the king in a cold pie.

Pepys, who had been imprisoned in the Tower in 1679 on a charge of giving the French information about the Navy (he eventually proved his innocence) was placed in the Gatehouse in 1690 on suspicion of being a supporter of ex-king James II, deposed in 1688, whom he had served faithfully as a civil servant. Pepys's stay in the Gatehouse was a short one and he was able to retire into private life without being persecuted again. The Gatehouse and Westminster Bridewell were not used to hold City prisoners, but were built to serve Westminster, as was Thieving Lane prison near the Sanctuary.

One kind of prison which was in existence as late as 1880 were the debtors' prisons which held all those in debt or, in some cases, in contempt. Conditions in debtors' prisons were in two classes. Anyone who could afford to pay the gaolers could buy themselves reasonable accommodation and perhaps considerable freedom of movement. If they could not, prisoners had to suffer appalling conditions. In Ludgate Prison, the debtors' prison built in the next gate south of Newgate, the poorest prisoners depended on charity for food. They were forced to hang baskets outside the prison into which passersby would place scraps. Other scraps came to them from the sheriffs' tables.

For the richer prisoners in Ludgate, conditions were comparatively decent, and the charges of the jailers were kept in bounds. From the late fourteenth century, freemen of the city had the privilege, if they were householders, of being imprisoned in Ludgate. However, conditions there deteriorated later and held no special advantages over those at other prisons. Ludgate was used for debtors for 350 years and towards the end of its role held about 100 debtors.

William Fennor, a pamphleteer, published in 1616 *The Counter's Commonwealth* in which he depicted life in the Wood Street Counters, one of the sheriffs' prisons for debtors. There were three Counters prisons at this time; they were in Poultry, Wood Street and at St. Margaret, Southwark. Poultry was the oldest and the building lasted until 1817. Wood Street was where Jonathan Wild spent four years at the start of his criminal career in the company of 'felons, roysterers and debtors of all ages'.

Fennor describes the different accommodation within Wood Street. The best apartments were on the Master's Side. The Knight's Ward had inferior quarters but was still comfortable in prison terms. But the Twopenny Ward and the Hole were no better than common gaols. Fennor met a bad-tempered gaoler who would not admit him to the Master's side without a fee:

'*Sir, if you mean to lie on this side, you must and shall pay me my fees, or, though you be no alderman, I will be so bold as to uncloak you.*' *I, seeing him so resolute, and myself loath to lie without a bed because it was so late, put mine arm into my pocket, which was so sore with the sergeants' gripping that I had much ado to pull two shillings out of it. That being discharged, like a brass viol he went grumbling upstairs with me and brought me to my lodgings, richly hung with cob-web lawn.*

A rich man could live very comfortably in the Counters once he had satisfied the demands of the gaolers. He had freedom to move about, receive friends, eat as he please and even run a trade. It was the poor prisoners who suffered in debtors' prisons and there were no public funds available for their welfare. However, conditions slightly improved in debtors' prisons, after the Insolvent Debtors Act, 1725, and after the trial of the Wardens of the Fleet in 1729.

The Fleet Prison was known to be in existence in the twelfth century, and it became the prison to which prisoners were committed by the Star Chamber. The Star Chamber was abolished in 1641 and the Fleet was then used by the Courts of Chancery, Exchequer, and Common Pleas. The Fleet, in common with the other debtors' prisons, had pressures on its accommodation during the ruin caused by the South Sea Bubble. It was easier, too, for traders to arrange to come out of debtors' prisons than for non-traders who were bankrupt. The insolvent Debtors Act was passed to give relief to non-traders who otherwise would spend many years or even a lifetime in prison before being able to secure their release. In 1725, therefore, many prisoners came out of the Fleet with stories and descriptions of life inside. For instance, a well-known smuggler who was in the Fleet was able to go to and fro as he pleased, even though he owed fines amounting to £30,000, because he had bribed the Deputy Governor. Handouts of this kind enabled debtors to live out of prison in certain defined areas known as the Liberty of the Rules. The Fleet, too, was popular for clandestine marriages which took place in the prison chapel but later in nearby inns and drink shops. These marriages were performed without licence by parson-debtors in return for a fee. However, these ceremonies were made illegal by the 1754 Marriage Act.

In the murder trial of ex-Warden of the Fleet, John Huggins, which was an indirect result of public concern with the prison, attention was drawn to the condition of the Strong Room on the Master's Side where Huggin's alleged victim, Edward Arne, had been placed. Huggins, who was acquitted, had paid £5,000 for his office.

The Strong Room was designed for obstinate prisoners, and each side in the prison had a room of this kind. On the Master's Side, it was a building 8 ft. by 11 ft. and 9 ft. high. According to one description, the Strong Room was

*. . . over the common sewer and next to the place where the prison ordure was deposited. It was damp, foul and noisome. The ostensible purpose of the place was the confinement of refractory prisoners. There they were flung, fettered, without fire or bedding, lying on the damp ground and surrounded by walls steaming with moisture. Its other use was as a mortuary for dead prisoners awaiting inquest. The only ventilation was by a hole over the door and one by the side big enough to pass a quart pot.**

Arne was unable to pay 'chummage', a levy extracted from new prisoners to buy drinks for all those confined in the same prison ward. He was therefore thrown naked into the Strong Room. Occasionally, Arne was flung some food, and a fellow prisoner managed to provide him with a mattress. One day, the door of the cell was left open, and Arne ran out into the hall. Filth and feathers from the mattress stuck to his skin so that he resembled a 'fantastic and repulsive bird'. The wretched man was marched back to the Strong Room and the Warden ordered the door to be locked again. It is not surprising that Arne died after such experiences.

Yet the Fleet had been rebuilt after the Great Fire. It was, of course, in a most insanitary position, being close to the east bank of that open sewer, the River Fleet. The prison was finally pulled down in 1844.

Another cluster of prisons was situated in Southwark: the Marshalsea, the King's Bench and Horsemonger Lane. Wat Tyler's men from Kent attacked both prisons in 1381 and later, Protestant martyrs were imprisoned and burnt the Marshalsea during the reign of Queen Mary. The Marshalsea was a royal prison and a convenient one to use to imprison anyone suspected of defying or ridiculing authority. Among its prisoners have been people accused of contempt, rioting, debt, libel and treason. Charles Dicken's father was imprisoned there for debt in 1824 and he gave his impressions of it in *Little Dorrit*. The Marshalsea was discontinued as a prison in 1842 and its inmates were transferred to the King's Bench.

---

* *Famous Trials* **by the Earl of Birkenhead (Hutchinson).**

Dickens also knew the King's Bench because it was not pulled down until 1880 when it was a military prison. In 1754, an Inquiry found that overcrowding in the prison caused 'extortions, cruelties, promiscuity, drunkeness and every irregularity'. However, nothing was done to ease the overcrowding because it would cut down on the income of the gaolers, who were reported to have made £800 a year each on the sales of drink alone ('120 gallons of gin were sold every week'). The King's Bench too, was surrounded by a dozen streets of 'Liberties' and rich prisoners could buy the freedom of this area. Among the famous prisoners here was John Wilkes the agitator and Smollett the novelist, both of whom were jailed here for libel. While imprisoned Smollett wrote his novel *Sir Launcelot Greaves*, in which he describes the unusually friendly atmosphere of the King's Bench:

> *Except the entrance, where the turnkeys keep watch and ward, there is nothing in the place that looks like a jail, or bears the least colour of restraint. The street is crowded with passengers. Tradesmen of all kinds here exercise their different professions. Hawkers of all sorts are admitted to call and vend their wares as in any open street of London. Here are butchers' stands, chandlers' shops, a surgery, a tap-house, well-frequented, and a public kitchen, in which provisions are dressed for all the prisoners gratis, at the expense of the publican. Here the voice of misery never complains; and, indeed, little else is to be heard but the sounds of mirth and jollity . . .*

Not so cheerful was Horsemonger Lane, the county gaol for Surrey from 1791 to 1879. All kinds of prisoners were received here, including murderers. Public executions used to take place on the roof over the main entrance and the inhabitants of the houses opposite used to rent their windows on these gruesome occasions. In contrast, James Leigh Hunt, the author, was imprisoned at Horsemonger Lane for two years in 1812 for describing the Prince Regent as a 'corpulent Adonis'. He was able to furnish his room elegantly with flowers, bookcases and his piano and receive his friends who included Byron, Shelley, Keats, Lamb and Hazlitt.

Another Southwark prison gave a word to the English language—the Clink, within the Liberty of the same name which was under the jurisdiction of the Bishop of Winchester. The Clink was once the prison in which people were confined who 'should babble, frey or break the peace on the said bank, or in the brothel houses'. Inmates from the Clink took part in the Gordon Riots of 1780. Some thirty years later, the prison was closed down.

Some London prisons had shorter lives. There was the New Prison, Clerkenwell, built in 1615, which Pepys mentions in 1668 when he reports the apprentice riot which was concerned with pulling down the brothels in Whetstone Park:

> . . . We heard a Justice of Peace this morning say to the King that he had been endeavouring to suppress this tumult, but could not: and that imprisoning some of them in the new prison at Clerkenwell, the rest did come and break open the prison and release them . . .

The New Prison became famous on odd occasions. For instance, it was one of the prisons from which Jack Sheppard escaped. Prisoners from here, too, were released during the Gordon Riots. In 1832, the prison was subject to an epidemic of cholera, caused by the reopening of the River Fleet as it was being converted into a proper sewer. The New Prison was also where the 1867 Fenian bomb outrage took place, killing 12 people. It was closed in 1877.

An even shorter-lived type of prison were the hulks anchored in the Thames. Old naval ships were first used as prisons when the war of American Independence and later the Napoleonic Wars made every ship valuable and every voyage transporting convicts to Australia and other Colonies dangerous. So prisoners who would have been transported were kept on old, damp and rotting vessels while they worked at dredging and other forms of hard labour. Hulks were liable to cholera and a well-publicised case was that of the *Justitia* moored off Woolwich which was infected in 1848. In 1841, the hulks, which had been thought of as a wartime measure, had 3,500 prisoners on board. At the end of the Crimean War, there were some 1,300.

The Tate Gallery is a popular attraction to art-lovers who come here to see the main national collection of British painting since 1500 and other exhibitions. But before the gallery was built in 1897, the site by the Thames was occupied by the huge and forbidding Millbank Penitentiary. Millbank, constructed in 1813–16, offered its prisoners a life of extreme dullness and loneliness. For the first half of their sentence, the prisoners were confined to their separate cells and forbidden to associate or work with their fellow inhabitants.

In the gaunt House of Correction at Cold Bath Fields, Mount Pleasant, prisoners had more contact with each other but were kept occupied with useless exercises such as the tread-mill, crank and shot-drill. Dickens knew the governor of Cold Bath Fields, whose policy was to exact severe retribution from the prisoners in silence, and was able to visit the prison. Both men and women were put on the treadmills, which consisted of 24 compartments in which the prisoners would tread down an individual wheel of twenty-four steps. A day treading meant that each prisoner would have 'climbed' nearly 9,000 feet. The crank was an unpopular prison pastime in which the prisoner had to turn a drum mounted on an axle with a crank-handle. The snag was that the drum was filled with sand or other loose material which made it very tiring to revolve. Shot-drill was confined to those below forty-five, because it was so exhausting. The prisoners had to pass twenty-four pound cannon balls to each other in a chain, with three yards between each man. Each shot-drill session lasted an hour and a quarter.

Two other forbidding and gloomy London prisons, long since demolished, were Wellclose Square and Whitecross Street. The former was originally for debtors and was connected with the high court of the liberties of the Tower of London. Military prisoners from the Peninsular War were once brought here. The latter, built in 1815, held 400 debtors and was eventually pulled down in 1870, when the prisoners were transferred to Holloway.

Many London prisons which are still in use were built during the nineteenth century: such as Pentonville, built in 1842; Wandsworth, opened in 1851; Holloway, rebuilt during the 1970's and first completed in 1851; Wormwood Scrubs, erected in 1890; and Brixton, built in 1820 and extended in 1898. Pentonville was built on a radiating plan copied from the Eastern Penitentiary at Philadelphia with 520 cells. While the prison was not too uncomfortable, the rules to isolate prisoners were. Masks were provided so that the inmates could not recognise each other. There were individual pews in the chapel so that the prisoners could not see each other. No one was allowed to communicate with any other prisoner and there were severe punishments if the rule was broken. Pentonville, then, was a place where many inmates went insane, or committed suicide.

At the turn of the century, prison reform had cleaned up London's prisons and society had slowly accepted that rehabilitation made a criminal a better citizen than did endless punishment. However, reform in certain respects will always be needed. The role of the London prisons has tended to be that of 'clearing houses' between the courts and provincial prisons such as Dartmoor and Parkhurst where long-term offenders are sent according to crime and sentence. But because the crime rate has risen, and the numbers of prison staff and prisons have not, most well-known London prisons suffer acute overcrowding. Perhaps it is an example of the wheel turning full circle. Overcrowding, with its attendant evils, was a characteristic of most common gaols in London's history before the last century. But prisons of all periods were never meant to be comfortable for criminals. As Coleridge wrote in *The Devil's Thoughts*:

> *As he went through Cold Bath Fields he saw*
> *A solitary cell;*
> *And the Devil was pleased, for it gave him a hint*
> *For improving his prisons in Hell*

CHAPTER EIGHT

CRIME AND PUNISHMENT

The King's ships captured me as I sailed, as I sailed,
The King's ships captured me, as I sailed,
The King's ships captured me, no more of piracy,
And no more to own the sea, as I sailed, as I sailed.

Now to Execution Dock I must go, I must go,
To Execution Dock I must go.
To the Execution Dock, put my head upon the block,
And no more God's laws I'll mock, as I fall, as I fall.

Take warning now by me, I must die, I must die,
Take warning now by me, I must die.
Take warning now by me, and shun all bad company,
Lest you go to hell with me as I die, as I die.

THESE THREE VERSES are from the broadside published on the occasion of the execution of Captain William Kidd for murder and piracy in 1701. Kidd's victim had been his gunner aboard his ship *The Adventure* and Kidd was charged with murdering him by striking him on the head with a bucket. About the same time, the Captain turned pirate and when he was captured in 1699, the first of several indictments against him was for the piratical capture of a ship called *The Quedagh Merchant*. Kidd and nine associates were tried at the Old Bailey and he and six of them were found guilty. They were sentenced to death and the sentence was carried out at the traditional place of execution for pirates, Execution Dock at Wapping Old Stairs.

The broadside suggests that Kidd was beheaded; in fact he was hanged and then gibbeted in chains within the sight of all the fleet, as all pirates in the sixteenth, seventeenth and eighteenth centuries were. There was a further custom, too. Pirates were hanged at the low water mark and their bodies remained there 'till three tides had overflowed them'. The idea was to discourage people on passing ships from taking up the profession of pirate. Pirates and occasionally highwaymen were hanged at Wapping until as late as 1735. They were also hanged on the other side of the Thames at the mouth of the river Neckinger which ran through Bermondsey. It is probable that the name may have come from the hangman's rope which was known as the Devil's Neckinger. The last hanging in chains took place in 1834.

Mr. Pepys was involved with the hanging of a pirate. In 1674, the captain of an Ostend pirate ship failed to salute the naval sloop *Woolwich*, and ended up on the Wapping gallows sentenced for both contempt and piracy. Pepys helped to prepare the warrant for the offender's execution and obtain a platoon of musketeers from the Tower to keep order at Execution Dock.

The hanging of pirates at Wapping, then, was a standard capital punishment in London. Hanging was also the most common method of executing Londoners condemned to death.

It was simple and effective and lent itself to judicial showmanship because a victim on the gallows was able to be seen by a large crowd. The law of the land approved of hanging not only because it was a deterrent to crime (albeit not a successful one) but also because it degraded the criminal to be treated so. People were no longer hanged in public after 1868 and it was abolished as a punishment for murder in 1965. There were other methods of capital punishment, too: beheading; burning alive; boiling in oil; hanging, drawing and quartering; and shooting. In the late tenth century, a woman found guilty of witchcraft was drowned off London Bridge. Many victims died as a result of torture to extract admissions of guilt, and there were several punishments such as branding which were painfully mutilating. These latter punishments were not, of course, capital ones, but were extensively used up to Tudor times, with exceptional penalties lasting until later centuries.* It was a general rule, too, that pregnant women should be spared execution until their children were born. So, if a condemned woman pleaded that she was with child, a panel of matrons was set up to examine the truth of the plea. On their word depended the immediate fate of the prisoner.

If the sixteenth century has a claim to be the cruellest age in London's history, it may be interesting to recall some of the punishments for comparatively minor crimes. In the eleventh century you could be blinded for killing deer but in the Elizabethan age you could lose a hand for stealing a sheep. If the magistrates considered you a rogue, they could order your ears to be burnt through or even to be removed if they believed you were a petty criminal or a troublemaker. If perjury was your line, you might end up with a P branded on your forehead and undergo a spell in the pillory. Forging important documents could earn you even more mutilating and burning of your face. Branding was not abolished until the 1750's. The pillory, stocks and ducking stool were used as public penances, designed to shame the offender. One example of a public penance was that inflicted on street-walkers. These ladies could have their hair cut off and be made to walk through the streets in their petticoats, accompanied by clanging basins and ringing handbells. If you were a tradesman who gave short measure or sold food unfit for consumption, you were either made to ride in a dung cart or suffer a similar fate to that of a butcher recorded by Henry Machyn in his *Diary of a Resident in London*, 1554:

> *The seventh day of March rode a butcher round about London, his face toward the horse tail, with half a lamb*

---

* Judicial torture in England ceased in 1640, but branding was not abolished until 1834, and the pillory was used up to 1837. Flogging continued until 1948 when it was limited to the offences of gross violence to prison officers, and mutiny and incitement to mutiny committed by prisoners. Flogging was an institutional punishment; for instance, in the nineteenth century it was a favourite and brutal sentence in the Army and Royal Navy, and in prisons, for many trivial offences. In 1823 it was revealed in the House of Lords that in seven years 6,959 floggings were administered in English prisons. In 1881, the passing of the Army Act restricted flogging in military prisons.

before and another behind, and veal and a calf borne
in front of him, upon a pole, raw.

A punishment which many Elizabethans considered had
potential merit but never materialised to any great extent was
the sentencing of vagabonds and the like to service as oarsmen
on royal galleys. Not only were there not enough galleys to
make the idea practical but it proved to be an expensive way
of dealing with prisoners. However, many convicts did go to
sea during the eighteenth and nineteenth centuries, when they
were transported to the Colonies. Transportation, initiated in
1717, came to an end in 1857, but not before thousands of
convicts had made an important contribution in founding
settlements in the Americas and Australasia. Two verses from
the nineteenth-century ballad *The Girl with the Black Velvet
Band* tell a contemporary story:

> *One day as we were a-walking*
> *A gentleman passed us by;*
> *I could see she was bent on some mischief*
> *By the rolling of her dark blue eye.*
> *Gold watch she picked from his pocket*
> *And slyly placed into my hand;*
> *I was taken in charge by a copper,*
> *Bad luck to that black velvet band.*
>
> *Before the Lord Mayor I was taken,*
> *'Your case, sir, I plainly can see,*
> *And, if I'm not greatly mistaken*
> *You're bound far over the sea.'*
> *It's over the dark and blue ocean,*
> *Far away to Van Diemen's Land,*
> *Way from my friends and relations*
> *And the girl with the black velvet band.*

Until 1827, the law considered that if a prisoner refused to
plead guilty or not guilty at the start of his trial, his refusal
meant that he was guilty. Previous to 1772, torture could be
used to make a man plead. There were several methods of
making a prisoner consent to do so. One was to tie the thumbs
together and twist the cord like a tourniquet, or even suspend

the prisoner by it. Another way was to order them to undergo the *peine forte et dure*, or pressing as it was called. Some prisoners, especially those without any hope of acquittal, preferred death by pressing for an important reason. The family of a convicted felon not only lost his possessions on his death but also their chances of succession. If a man was pressed to death, he would die unconvicted and his family would not be deprived of their property or their rights.

What exactly was the *peine forte et dure* as carried out in Newgate? When Major George Strangeways was directed to undergo the torture in the Press Yard after refusing to plead at his trial for murder in 1658, the Court ordered:

> *That the prisoner be sent back to the place from whence he came and there put into a mean room where no light can enter, that he be laid upon his back with his body bare, save something to cover his privy parts, that his arms be stretched forth with a cord, one to each side of the prison, and in like manner his legs shall be used, that upon his body shall be laid as much iron and stone as he can bear and more, that the first day he shall have three morsels of barley bread and the next day he shall drink thrice of the water in the next channel to the prison door, but no fountain or spring water, and this shall be his punishment till he dies.*

In fact, the Major was dead within ten minutes. A square wooden frame was laid across his body and iron weights were

The effects on his skin were horrible, the diagonal pink lines glowing scarlet and running into one another till there was a broad scarlet band which quivered and flushed and changed colour, but there was no blood. Twenty-four, twenty-five lashes and then came a loud voice 'Stop' and the prisoner was cut loose to walk quietly away from the post.

From a description of a flogging at Newgate in 1871. *The Illustrated Police News.*

put on it. He had asked his friends to add their weight to the frame which they did. The combined weight soon ended his suffering, and he died unconvicted of a capital felony.

One of the oldest punishments of all is flogging, which in the form of birching has aroused controversy in modern times. Flogging, of course, was not confined solely to prisons, but was used to keep discipline in many institutions, more often than not military as well as educational. William Calcraft, the city's official executioner from 1828 to 1871, was paid half-a-crown a time for flogging and was given a small allowance for birches and cats-o'-nine-tails. In 1871, a typical sentence for robbery with violence would be seven years penal servitude, seven years police supervision together with thirty lashes with the cat-o'-nine-tails. Of all democratic countries in Europe, Britain is the only one to allow whipping in schools.

But as late as 1820 there were still more than two hundred crimes punishable by death including picking a pocket of more than a shilling, or stealing goods worth more than 25p from a shop. To most offenders, this meant death by hanging. To the city, it meant that there was a high incidence of hanging. For instance, ninety-six people were executed at Newgate during 1785, twenty of them on one day (in 1864, Newgate had eight hangings out of a national total of 19; just over a century later, hanging was abolished). Major reform in capital punishment came in 1837 when the government abolished the death penalty for stealing, forgery, inciting to mutiny, armed smuggling and aiding the escape of criminals. At one stroke, the number of executions was reduced by almost two-thirds.

As a general custom, convicted felons and vagrants were hanged at recognised places of execution. But magistrates could, and did, order an execution to take place near the scene of the crime. Pepys records one instance in 1664:

> *Up, and after sending my wife to my aunt Wright's to get a place to see Turner hanged, I to the 'Change; and seeing people flock in the City, I enquired, and found that Turner was not yet hanged. And so I went among them to Leadenhall Street, at the end of Lyme Street, near where the robbery was done; and to St. Mary Axe, where he lived. And there I got for a shilling to stand upon the wheel of a cart, in great pain, above an hour*

before the execution was done; he delaying the time by long discourses and prayers one after another, in hopes of a reprieve; but none come, and at last was flung off the ladder in his cloak. A comely-looked man he was, and kept his countenance to the end: I was sorry to see him.

Pepys exemplifies the morbid interest shown by all classes of citizen in watching executions. (Two men of exceptional necrophily were George Selwyn in the eighteenth century and the Marquis of Waterford in the nineteenth.) The gallows in Pepys's time consisted of a crossbeam either supported on two posts or extending, braced, from one post. The ladder leant against the crossbeam. The condemned person had to climb the ladder because the noose was on a short piece of rope. This was so that the prisoner could swing in view of the witnessing crowds. The hangman preceded his pinioned victim up the ladder in order to adjust the noose. At this stage, some prisoners elected to address the crowd, either to repent or praise their crimes or to declaim their innocence. Usually a clergyman was at hand with last-minute prayer and exhortation. Then the condemned

Being bade to confess his treason, for so the Queen would doubtless pardon him, Jennings answered, 'I know not ever to have offended her. If to say Mass be treason, I confess I have done it and glory in it.' These words so enraged Topcliffe (the man who arrested Jennings) that he refused him leave to say any more, scarcely even to recite the *Pater noster*, but caused him to be turned off the ladder and the rope immediately cut. Jennings was thus thrown on his feet, but the hangman tripped up his heels, cut off his members and embowelled him. In this agony Jennings began to call on St. Gregory to the great astonishment of the hangman, who cried out with a loud voice, 'God's wounds! his heart is in my hand and yet Gregory is in his mouth'.

A description of the execution of the Jesuit Edmund Jennings in December, 1591. From *The Elizabethan Journals* by G. B. Harrison (Routledge & Kegan Paul 1938).

person was blindfolded and 'turned off' the ladder by the hangman who was ready to cut the rope if, say, a reprieve arrived. Sometimes the prisoner would jump off the ladder unassisted.

Climbing the ladder had many disadvantages, particularly if the victim was drunk or in a fainting condition. With the eighteenth century came a change of technique. A cart was used instead of the ladder and was backed underneath the cross-beam of the gallows, acting as a platform on which the criminal stood. When the Ordinary—the chaplain—had finished his ministrations, the noose was adjusted and the white cap drawn over the culprit's face. Then the hangman lashed the horses and drove the cart away from under the victim's feet, leaving him swinging and strangling on the end of the rope. Once the use of the cart was established, most gallows were built lower than previously.

Before 1400, most of the city's hangings took place in Cheapside, as the city's most important street. The particular point of execution was at the Standard, near where King Street crosses Cheapside. Cheapside was more than a thoroughfare; it was a market and a place for popular gatherings such as carnivals, sports, celebrations—and executions. As well as the gallows, a well-known pillory was situated in Cheapside. South of the Thames, a gallows was set up on the Kent Road at St. Thomas's Waterings. Travellers approaching London from the south east would be reminded by the sight of the gallows to keep on the side of the law. The authorities, too, could count on small crowds at the site. John Penry, condemned for sedition, was hanged at St. Thomas's Waterings in 1593 'with little warning and few spectators, lest he should have raised some tumult, either in going to the gallows or upon the ladder'. St. Thomas's Waterings was a predecessor as a place of execution for Surrey criminals to Horsemonger Lane prison.

London's famous place of execution, where hangings became a spectacle, was Tyburn, near to the present-day Marble Arch. The gallows was situated at or near the crossroads of two Roman roads—Watling Street, running northwest, and the Bath Road, heading west. Why Tyburn was chosen as an execution site is not clear, as the gallows was some two and a half miles from Newgate. But after 1400, nearly every common criminal who was condemned to death in the city made this last journey. The gallows was known as Tyburn Tree, so it is possible that at one time there was a great tree here which was a well-known landmark. One theory suggests that the original 'Tyburn trees' were the elms growing beside the river Tyburn on which criminals were strung. In the early eighteenth century, the gallows in Deadly Never Green, which was one name for Tyburn, appeared to be a permanent structure. It took the form of three upright posts, forming a triangle and joined with beams at the top. Eight bodies could swing side by side from each of the three beams. The site of this erection can be seen at Marble Arch, marked by a plaque set in the ground.

Tyburn's heyday was in the eighteenth century, before the authorities built the new Newgate and made that the official place of execution in 1783. The procedure for a day's hanging at Tyburn hardly ever varied at this time. People were hanged in batches, on one of the eight hanging days a year. Each of these, needless to say, was a public holiday. So about every six weeks, the condemned would be prepared at Newgate. These verses from *The Black Dog of Newgate* give some idea of the scene:

The sermon ended, the men condemned to die,
Taking their leaves of their acquainted friends,
With sorry looks, pacing their steps, they ply
Down to a hall where for them there attends
A man of office who, to daunt life's hopes,
Doth cord their hands and scarf their necks with ropes.

Thus roped and corded, they descend the stairs:
Newgate's black dog bestirs to play his part,
And does not cease for to augment their cares,
Willing the carman to set near his cart.
Which done, these men, with fear of death o'erhanging,
Bound to the cart are carried to be hanged.

Each condemned man travelled with his coffin in the cart with him or in a following cart. Sometimes, the condemned wore shrouds as did Stephen Gardner executed in 1724. In 1605, Robert Dowe provided a fund for the ringing of a hand-bell outside the Condemned Hold on the night before a hanging day with the intention of making the condemned felons repent before they set out for Tyburn. Not everyone travelled in the carts. In 1760, Earl Ferrers—claiming that his wife was responsible for his misfortunes—drove from the Tower of Tyburn in his landau to be hanged for murdering his steward in his wedding clothes of white silk trimmed with silver braid.

Lord Ferrers was the only peer of the realm ever to hang at Tyburn. The Sheriffs decided to 'make the most of the opportunity of pageantry'. Thus a large parade set out from the Tower of London on the morning of May 5th. Horace Bleackley describes it in *The Hangmen of England*:

> *First marched a very large body of constables from the county of Middlesex, preceded by one of the high constables. Then came two parties of the Grenadier Guards, one mounted, the other on foot, followed by Sheriff Errington in the official chariot. Next in order was Lord Ferrers' carriage and six, surrounded by a company of horse soldiers and more of the Grenadier Guards. Sheriff Vaillant followed in his public carriage, and the mourning coach (rejected by Ferrers) brought up the rear, along with a hearse and six horses, which was to convey his lordship's corpse to the dissecting room at Surgeons' Hall.*

The Triple Tree, now an 'inconvenient obstacle', had been pulled down seven months previously in favour of a 'new Moving Gallows' which could be taken by cart to Tyburn on

~~~~~~

> His countenance ghastly, fearful, grim, and pale,
> His foamy mouth still gapeth for his prey;
> With tiger's teeth he spares none to assail,
> His lips hell-gates, o'erpainted with decay,
> His tongue the clapper, sounding woeful knell,
> Tolling poor men to ring a peal in hell.

From *The Black Dog of Newgate* by Luke Hutton, 1596. A note from the 1638 edition: 'It was a walking spirit in the likeness of a black dog gliding up and down the streets a little before the time of execution, and in the night while the sessions continued...'

~~~~~~

hanging days. But the sheriffs had prepared a new and elaborate scaffold for Lord Ferrers. Beneath the crossbeam was a little raised stage which could be lowered to leave the criminal suspended. Everything was covered with black baize. Ferrers was guided to the stage where his arms were bound with a black silk sash, 'for a common cord could not be used upon a man of his rank'. After an unseemly squabble between the hangman, Thomas Turlis, and his assistant over the gratuity of five guineas offered by Ferrers, the execution took place. Horace Walpole reported it:

> *When the rope was put around his neck, he turned pale, but recovered his countenance instantly, and was but seven minutes from leaving the coach, to the signal given for striking the stage. As the machine was new, they were not ready at it: his toes touched it, and he suffered a little, having had time, by their bungling, to raise his cap; but the executioner pulled it down again, and they pulled his legs, so that he was soon out of pain, and quite dead in four minutes.*

Lord Ferrer's execution was highly popular with the Tyburn mob. So too were those of the twin brothers Robert and Daniel Perreau, hanged for forgery in 1776. Forgery, at that time, was an offence which almost automatically meant death. Their case aroused enormous interest because they accused Daniel's mistress, Mrs. Margaret Caroline Rudd, of being responsible for the forgeries. But Mrs. Rudd was acquitted and the brothers condemned. The largest crowd since that present at the Ferrers's hanging thronged to Tyburn. An unusual feature of the execution was that two of the seven convicts in the hanging batch that day were Jewish housebreakers. The gallows was a double one, so that the five Christians could be hanged on one beam and the Jews on the other. The twins held hands as they died.

By far the greatest crowd-puller was the Reverend William Dodd, D.D., who was also hanged for forgery, in 1777. He was a popular preacher and was known as the 'Macaroni Parson' because of his dandyism. Dr. Samuel Johnson attempted to gain the Doctor a pardon but to no avail. On the day of the execution, the authorities brought 2,000 soldiers into Hyde

Park to keep order. The crowd that gathered was the largest ever known for such an occasion. Every window between Newgate and Tyburn was filled with spectators and all along the route people stood many rows deep. An eyewitness remarked that when the hangman, Edward Dennis, was about to place the noose around Dodd's neck, the latter removed his wig, exposing his bald, shaved head. It began to rain at this point, so somebody on the scaffold held an umbrella over the Doctor even though he had only a few moments to live.

The two-mile journey to Tyburn took about an hour, depending on the popularity of the condemned travellers and the curiosity of the mob. A crowd of 200,000 turned out to see Jack Sheppard on his execution day and Lord Ferrers's journey took three hours from the Tower because there were so many people on the route. All the processions had to pass by the Church of the Holy Sepulchre, now in Newgate Street. The Church sexton often used to present a bunch of flowers to each criminal with an exhortation as he went on his way. The way then led down into the valley of the Fleet, across the river and up to Holborn Hill by St. Andrew's Church. This valley was not bridged until the building of Holborn Viaduct in the 1860's. After passing along High Holborn, there was a brief stop at The Bowl, St. Giles, where the prisoners received a customary free bowl of ale. From St. Giles, the Oxford Road led straight to Tyburn.

There was always a huge crowd at the Tree and hawkers did excellent business selling oranges, pies, drink and verses and speeches of condemned murderers. There were plenty of pickpockets, too, and the whole occasion resembled a sporting occasion. There was even a grandstand known as Mother Proctor's Pews (after the farmer's widow who rented it out) where the best people would sit. The execution of a personality such as James M'Lean the highwayman would attract many parties of the aristocracy. In the next century, respectable people would withdraw from watching executions which meant that the behaviour of the spectators grew less and less orderly.

When a cart carrying a condemned man arrived from Newgate, it would drive under the 'tripod' gallows. If the criminal was popular with the crowd as a famous highwayman would be, the cart would be full of bouquets of flowers, given to him on the way. If he was unpopular, as Jonathan Wild was, the spectators lining the route would pelt him with filth. At Tyburn, the mood of the crowd determined the speed of the hangman's work. If the mob was hostile to a condemned man, the hangman was quick to give that man immediate attention. It was customary for the condemned to prepare a speech to give from the gallows, but on many occasions the crowd was too noisy for the victim to be heard. Others preferred to die in silence. The hangman's task was comparatively easy; all he had to do was to adjust the noose and order the cart to be driven away. Wild managed to pick the ordinary's pockets before the horses moved away.

After an hour or so, the bodies would be cut down. Those of common criminals would be taken to the Surgeons' Hall in the Old Bailey for dissection. If a hanged man had friends willing enough, they would be permitted to try and revive him. Dr. Dodd's friends organised a waiting coach and a hot bath and a surgeon at Goodge Street, but not only was the coach delayed by the crowded streets but also the Doctor was truly dead. Experiments had already started with the drop method of hanging, which killed quickly by dislocating the neck. In this method, a handle was pulled which opened trap doors under the victim who dropped through the scaffold for a few feet to be stopped short by the rope around his neck.

In 1783, Tyburn ceased to be a place of execution on the completion of the new Newgate prison. Thereafter, all criminals convicted of capital crimes committed in the City of London or the County of Middlesex were hanged there. There were

Dr. Scarborough took some of his friends, and I went with them, to see the body of a lusty fellow, a seaman, that was hanged for a robbery. It seems one Dillon, of a great family, was, after much endeavours to have saved him, hanged with a silken halter this Sessions, (of his own preparing,) not for honour only, but it being soft and sleek it do slip close and kills, that is strangles presently: whereas, a stiff one do not come so close together, and so the party may live the longer before killed.

Pepys's Diary, 27th February, 1663.

pertinent reasons for the transfer of function. The processions to Tyburn had become 'an obstacle to traffic and a hindrance to business'. Also, residents in the Tyburn neighbourhood which had now become fashionable not only disliked the mobs which assembled for the executions but also disapproved of the gallows being so close to their houses.

With the move of executions to Newgate, the drop method became generally accepted. However, not every hangman in this location mastered the technique efficiently. For instance, William Calcraft who became City Executioner in 1829 was a 'short-drop' man and was firm in his belief that a drop of two or three feet was enough to kill a man painlessly. Even his last victim after some forty years as public hangman underwent considerable suffering. Calcraft's successor in 1874, William Marwood, made hanging an art. He would give his victims the

The accustomed signal having been given, the drop sank; but the wretched man, instead of falling with it, suddenly jumped upon the platform, and seizing the cord around his throat with his hands, which he had sufficiently loosened by the violence of his struggles, he made an effort to prolong that life to which he seemed to be so strongly attached. At this moment the spectacle was horrifying in the extreme. The convict was partly suspended and partly resting on the platform. During his exertions his tongue had been forced from his mouth and the convulsions of his body and the contortions of his face were truly appalling. The cries from the crowd were of a frightful description, and they continued until the executioner had forced the wretched man's hand from the cord and having removed his feet from the platform, had suffered his whole weight to be sustained by the rope. The distortions of his countenance could even now be seen by the crowd, and as he remained suspended with his face uncovered, the spectacle was terrific. The hangman at length terminated his sufferings by hanging to his legs, and the unhappy wretch was seen to struggle no more.

Description of the execution of Charles White at Newgate, 1827. Camden Pelham, *Chronicles of Crime*, 1887.

The 'New Drop' at Newgate, on which a dozen criminals could be hanged at the same time.

longest drop necessary, according to their weight, to cause instantaneous death.

The new execution site at Newgate was in front of the prison in Old Bailey, a few yards away from the main gate and by a side door through which the condemned man and the prison officials would emerge to mount the scaffold. The scaffold itself was 'portable'; it was positioned for each execution outside the Debtor's Door. Twelve criminals could be dispatched at a time on it. Sometimes a crowd of over fifty thousand people would crush into the Old Bailey to watch the proceedings. A crowd of this size watched the hanging of the train murderer Franz Müller as late as 1864.

In 1807 thirty people were killed when the vast crowd pressed and pushed towards the scaffold on which two convicts, John Holloway and James Haggerty, were hanged. The greatest crowd ever reported in the Old Bailey was that at the execution of Henry Fauntleroy, the banker, hanged for forgery in 1824. As well as the spectators in the street, the windows and roofs of buildings overlooking the scaffold were jammed with people. After the execution, the ordinary of Newgate, the Rev. Horace Salusbury Cotton, was censured by the authorities for 'harrowing the prisoner's feelings unnecessarily'. A contemporary report states that barrels of beer were brought to executions and their contents sold with other refreshments to the waiting crowd which sang songs such as:

> *Oh my!*
> *Think I've got to die.*

Richer spectators could hire a window for twenty guineas at the Magpie and Stump pub which was opposite the place of execution. The pub, in its rebuilt form, is still there in the Old Bailey.

A typical execution party consisted of the two sheriffs, the under-sheriffs, the governor of Newgate, the prison surgeon, the ordinary and representatives of the press who would assemble in the Large Room.

The arrival of the condemned man was preceded by the sound of clanking fetters. Once in the room, the fetters would be removed by the prison smith using a hammer. Then the Yeoman of the Halter bound his arms close to his body above his elbow.

The ordinary would then read from his prayer book with the prisoner. Religious consolation was interrupted when the Sheriffs approached the prisoner to ask whether he had any messages or last requests. Then, on checking the time, the procession would move off towards the Debtor's Door. Executions usually took place at eight o'clock on Monday mornings. One of 'The Bells of Old Bailey', in St. Selpulchre's Church was always tolled for the occasion until 1890. Dickens described the scene just before eight in *Oliver Twist*:

> *A great multitude had already assembled; the windows were filled with people, smoking and playing cards to beguile the time; the crowd were pushing, quarrelling, and joking. Everything told of life and animation, but one dark cluster of objects in the very centre of all— the black stage, the cross-beam, the rope, and all the hideous apparatus of death.*

The rope would be attached to the crossbeam by a short chain and under it was the trap, operated by a lever which released a draw bar under the doors. Sometimes the 'great multitude' was reduced in size if another execution was taking place elsewhere in London at the same time. This happened for instance, with almost simultaneous executions at Newgate and Horsemonger Lane Gaol on 19th October 1867.

When eight o'clock came, the prison bell would toll briefly, and the prisoner would emerge in front of the crowd, accompanied by the executioner and the ordinary. Then a huge roar rose from the crowd.

William Marwood was as well known a figure in late Victorian England as W. G. Grace, and was the subject of one of those conundrums which his contemporaries found so diverting. 'If Pa killed Ma, who'd kill Pa?' The answer, of course, was 'Marwood'. He succeeded Calcraft as public hangman in 1874. Calcraft, a kindly man, fond of pigeons and children, had held office for forty-five years.

Giles St. Aubyn, *Infamous Victorians* (Constable 1971).

'Hats off! Hats off!'

Every spectator standing in the packed Old Bailey was anxious that he got a good view of the proceedings. The small party would then ascend the scaffold where the victim would be blindfolded with a white cap and the rope adjusted round his neck and through the chain. The executioner then left the scaffold to pull the trap lever. The body would hang for an hour before being confined within the scaffold. After 1868, Newgate executions took place in 'a dismal shed standing in one corner' within the walls, out of the morbid public gaze.

One industry which was still thriving on murders and executions in the mid-nineteenth century was that of the street-ballad and the Last Dying Speech and Confession. These were usually printed in the Seven Dials area by the Pitts or Catnach presses, and sales of a ballad on a sensational murder could reach the quarter-million mark.

In *London Labour and the London Poor*, Mayhew published returns of the numbers of execution broadsheets sold 'relating to principal executions of late':

Of Rush	*2,500,000*	*Of Greenacre*	*1,666,000*
Of the Mannings	*2,500,000*	*Of Good*	*1,650,000*
Of Courvoisier	*1,666,000*	*Of Corder*	*1,650,000*

Rush, a farmer, was hanged at Norwich in 1849 for shooting his landlord; Greenacre, a Southwark tradesman, murdered and dismembered Hannah Brown for which crime he was hanged in 1837; and Corder, another farmer, was hanged at Bury St. Edmunds in 1828 for shooting his mistress.

Mayhew also gave examples of murder literature, such as the following title page from a pamphlet sold in London:

Founded on Facts

THE WHITBY TRADGEDY
or
The Gambler's Fate

Containing the Lives of Joseph Carr, aged 21, and his sweetheart, Maria Leslie, aged 19, who were found dead, lying by each other, on the morning of the 23rd

*of May. Maria was on her road to Town to buy some
Ribbon, &c., for her Wedding Day, when her lover in
a state of intoxication fired at her, and then run to rob
his prey, but finding it to be his Sweetheart, reloaded
his Gun, placed the Muzzle to his Mouth, and blew out
his Brains, all through cursed Cards, Drink, &c. Also
an affectionate Copy of Verses.*

But the popularity of these ballads, sheets, and pamphlets
faded away with the shutting away of executions, the growth
of daily newspapers, the demise of prisons such as Newgate
and Horsemonger Lane and the introduction of new prisons
such as Pentonville and Wandsworth where hanging took place
until it was abolished.

At Wandsworth, the condemned cell was built next to the
execution shed with a thin metal sliding wall between them.
The trap consisted of heavy oak doors which would be marked
with chalk to show where the condemned man should stand.
The length of rope required would be decided by reference to
a table relating to human height and weight. The rope, attached
to its short chain hanging from the beam, would be coiled and
held in place by a piece of thread. Over the span of a century,
the procedure for a hanging remained the same.

~~~~~~

**When the sun rose brightly—as it did—it gilded thousands upon
thousands of upturned faces, so inexpressibly odious in their
brutal mirth or callousness, that a man had cause to feel ashamed
of the shape he wore, and to shrink from himself, as fashioned in
the image of the devil. When the two miserable creatures who
attracted all this ghastly sight about them were turned quivering
into the air, there was no more emotion, no more pity, no more
thought that two immortal souls had gone to judgement, no more
restraint in any of the previous obscenities, than if the name of
Christ had never been heard in this world . . .**

**Charles Dickens in a letter to *The Times* after attending the
public execution of Mr. and Mrs. George Manning at Horsemonger Lane Gaol, 13th November, 1849.**

~~~~~~

Before capital punishment was abolished in Britain, only a few seconds elapsed from the moment the executioner entered the condemned cell just before eight o'clock in the morning to the death of the condemned prisoner. Before the executioner arrived, the prisoner was offered brandy. Then the executioner came in with his assistant who strapped the prisoner's arms behind his back. Then the condemned man walked the few steps to the gallows between two warders. In position, the executioner placed a white cap over the criminal's head and face and fixed the noose in the right position, while his assistant pinioned the prisoner's legs. With these preparations complete, both officials stepped back and the executioner immediately released the lever operating the trap doors, through which the prisoner fell to his death.

One form of capital punishment lasted for just three hundred and sixty years and was reserved for people of high rank. This was beheading with an axe. Most beheadings were therefore memorable occasions. Lord Derwentwater, executed in 1715 for supporting the Old Pretender, is commemorated in a ballad, a verse of which could apply to most victims of the axe:

> He laid his head upon the block
> The axe was sharp and strong;
> The stroke that cut his sufferings short
> His memory cherished long.

Most victims were beheaded on Tower Hill or within the Tower on Tower Green as a special privilege, but there were exceptions. To give two, Charles I was beheaded at Whitehall Palace in 1649 and Sir Walter Raleigh suffered the same fate in 1618 at Old Palace Yard, Westminster.

Beheading was a military punishment fashionable with the Romans and William the Conqueror introduced it into Britain in 1076 when Waltheof, Earl of Huntingdon, was executed by this method. While Wat Tyler's men beheaded some victims on Tower Hill, the first official execution here was that of Sir Simon Burley in 1387. Burley, who was over 80, was Lord Chancellor and former tutor to Richard II. Between his execution and the last to take place, that of Lord Lovat in 1747, some seventy-five people were known to have been beheaded on Tower Hill. There was a permanent scaffold here and this had to be repaired from time to time. When Thomas Howard, Duke of Norfolk, was executed in 1572, there had been no executions for twelve years and the timbers of the scaffold had rotted. The scaffold had to be rebuilt for the occasion. In its basic form, the scaffold was about five feet high and made from rough planks. Railings draped in black surrounded it. On the side nearest the buildings on Tower Hill were wooden steps. Straw covered most of the scaffold, and a basket half filled with sawdust was placed in front of the block so that the victim's head fell into it.

Tower Green saw the beheadings of just seven people, five of them women. The victims were Lord Hastings (1483), Anne Boleyn (1536), the Countess of Salisbury (1541), Catharine Howard (1542), Viscountess Rochford (1542), Lady Jane Grey (1554), and the Earl of Essex (1601). Lord Hastings was a summary victim of Richard, Duke of Gloucester, and was rushed out of a council meeting in the White Tower to be beheaded on a baulk of timber. Anne Boleyn, second wife of Henry VIII, was executed for allegedly committing adultery and incest. She asked to die by the sword and not by the axe, and so a French executioner was hired for the event. He wore a mask and a suit of black while Anne wore a red robe. No one had provided a coffin so the ex-queen was buried in an old arrow chest.

The seventy-year-old Countess of Salisbury was executed for treason. So indeed was Catharine Howard, Henry VIII's fifth wife, who was charged with her accomplice Lady Rochford. The King had turned against Catharine because of her affair with Thomas Culpepper after her royal marriage. Catharine asked for a rehearsal with the block so that the execution went off smoothly. Lady Jane Grey was the figurehead of a plot to deprive Mary Tudor of the throne when her brother Edward VI died. The plot failed but Mary had no intention of executing Jane Grey. Unfortunately for Jane, the rebellion led by Thomas Wyatt brought about a change of mind and Jane (a focal point for rebellion) could no longer be left alive.

The Earl of Essex had fallen from Queen Elizabeth's favour and had instigated a plot to ensure that James VI of Scotland succeeded Elizabeth. Essex was beheaded dressed entirely in black (except for a scarlet waistcoat) and the executioner was one Derrick, whose talents as a hangman were marked by the passing of his name into the English language to describe 'a stationary crane employing hoisting tackle rigged at the end of a boom or lifting jib'. The unfortunate Earl had to lie down to fit his neck on the low block. Having done so, Derrick made him get up again to remove his doublet which he considered might obstruct the axe. When Essex laid his head on the block again, Derrick took three blows to decapitate him. Later, Derrick was attacked by a large crowd waiting outside the Tower and had to be rescued by the Sheriffs 'else he had been murdered'.

But Derrick was not the only well-known headsman who showed incompetence at times. Jack Ketch had to strike Lord William Russell 'four or five times' at his execution in Lincoln's Inn Fields in 1683. Russell had been condemned for allegedly taking part in the Rye House Plot to murder Charles II and his brother James, Duke of York. Two years later on Tower Hill, Ketch used a blunt axe on the Duke of Monmouth, leader of the failed uprising to depose James after he became James II. Monmouth had been subjected at the scaffold to the attentions of four clergymen who wanted him to regret his rebellion in public. While he regretted the bloodshed, he refused to commit himself further, despite two more attempts by the divines to make him confess more. Then Monmouth felt the edge of Ketch's axe and feared it was not sharp enough to cut his head off at one stroke. He was right. After the first blow, Monmouth got to his feet with a look of reproach. Ketch tried again—and again. The crowd roared in anger. Ketch threw down his axe and told the Sheriffs to do the job themselves. The Sheriffs ordered Ketch to finish his work. Which he did, with the help of a knife.

It was not surprising that Ketch was imprisoned in Bridewell a year later for insulting a Sheriff. But Ketch was back in his job within two years. His successor was hanged at Tyburn. A century before, one Cratwell, a London hangman, was hanged at Clerkenwell for robbing a booth at Bartholomew Fair. Between Derrick and Ketch came Gregory and Richard Brandon and Edward Dun, who achieved nothing like the same notoriety, with the possible exception of Richard Brandon who was jailed for bigamy in 1641.

On Tower Hill today, the site of the scaffold is marked by a granite slab marked

Site of the ancient Scaffold. Here the Earl of Kilmarnock and Lord Balmerino suffered, 18th August, 1746.

Except for Lord Lovat, these lords were the last people to be executed by beheading in London. They were supporters of Prince Charles Edward, the Young Pretender, and had been captured after the '45' rebellion had been smashed at the battle of Culloden. Balmerino, 58, and Kilmarnock, 42, were tried in Westminster Hall and sentenced to death. A contemporary print shows a huge crowd assembled to watch the proceedings. Many of the spectators were in viewing stands, some of which had several tiers. According to *The Gentleman's Magazine* for August 1746, a thousand foot-guards, a troop of life-guards and a troop of horse-grenadiers were 'posted in lines from the Tower to the Scaffold, and all round it'. There were also lines of troops to keep a passageway between the scaffold and the house called the Transport Office on the west side of Tower Hill. The Transport Office was used as a kind of waiting room for prisoners before their execution. Balmerino and Kilmarnock were brought here after the Sheriffs had formally collected them from the Tower. As *The Gentleman's Magazine* reported, the Sheriffs went to the Bulwark Gate

. . . and after knocking at it some time, a warder within asked, who's there? *the officer without replied,* the sheriffs *of* London *and* Middlesex. *The warder then asked,* what do they want? *the officer answered,* the bodies of *William* earl of *Kilmarnock,* and *Arthur* lord *Balmerino; upon which the warder within said,* I will go and inform the lieutenant of the *Tower, and in about 10 minutes the lieut. of the* Tower *with the earl of* Kilmarnock, *and major* White *with lord* Balmerino, *guarded by several of the warders, came to the gate, the prisoners were then delivered to the sheriffs, who gave proper receipts for their bodies to the lieutenant, who, as is usual, said,* God bless KING GEORGE; *to*

which the earl of Kilmarnock *assented by a bow, and
the lord* Balmerino *said,* God bless King J——s.

There is no report of the reaction to Balmerino's remark
which referred to James Edward Stuart, the Old Pretender,
whom Jacobites called James III and who was now 58. It could
not have been popular. A long procession which included two
hearses and a mourning coach took the two peers to the
Transport Office. When Kilmarnock came out on to the scaffold
from the Transport Office, it was the executioner, John Thrift,
whose nerve failed, not his, according to the *Gentlemen's
Magazine*:

> *The executioner, who before had something adminis-
> tered to keep him from fainting, was so affected by his
> lordship's distress, and the awfulness of the scene that,
> on asking his forgiveness, he burst into tears. My Lord
> bade him take courage, giving him at the same time a
> purse with five guineas.*

It was very unlikely that everyone in the vast throng saw the
executions clearly. However, the *Newgate Calendar* reported
that the colonel of the guard, or the sheriffs, ordered the black
baize which hung over the railings of the scaffold to be 'turned
up, so that the people might see all the circumstances of the
execution'. In the same report, the death of Lord Kilmarnock
was described as follows:

> *In about two minutes (the time he before fixed) after he
> kneeled down, his lordship dropping his handkerchief,
> the executioner at once severed his head from his body,
> except only a small part of the skin, which was
> immediately divided by a gentle stroke.*

But with Lord Balmerino . . .

> *The blow was not given with strength enough to wound
> him very deeply; on which it seemed as if he made an
> effort to turn his head towards the executioner . . . A
> second blow immediately succeeding the first rendered
> him, however, quite insensible, and a third finished the
> work.*

In 1662, Pepys went to Tower Hill for the execution of Sir Henry Vane, ex-Parliamentarian, and he could not see, even from a vantage point.

> *14th June. About 11 o'clock, having a room got ready for us, we all went out to the Tower-hill; and there, over against the scaffold, made on purpose this day, saw Sir Henry Vane brought. A very great press of people. He made a long speech, many times interrupted by the Sheriffe and others there; and they would have taken his paper out of his hand, but he would not let it go. But they caused all the books of those that writ after him to be given the Sheriffe; and the trumpets were brought under the scaffold that he might not be heard. Then he prayed, and so fitted himself, and received the blow; but the scaffold was so crowded that we could not see it.*

But the spectacle of beheading ended in 1747 with the execution of Simon, Lord Lovat. He, too, was a Jacobite peer, and like Sir Simon Burley, the first man to be beheaded on Tower Hill, was over eighty years old. As usual, an enormous gathering of spectators crowded round the scaffold. Suddenly, one of the viewing stands collapsed and several people were killed, which pleased the old man. He was buried in the Chapel of St. Peter ad Vincula in the Tower, and George Selwyn, the necrophilist, was present when the undertakers stitched his head on to his body.

A method of capital punishment which lasted for even a shorter period than beheading was burning at the stake. This was the ultimate penalty inflicted by the Inquisition in Europe for heresy against the Roman Catholic Church. The infamous Grand Inquisitor of Spain, Torquemada, was reputed to have ordered the burning alive of about 200 people in the fifteenth century. Pope Paul III persecuted Italian Protestants with the Inquisition in 1542. So it was not surprising that Queen Mary Tudor's reign, especially after her marriage to Philip of Spain in 1555, should emulate this example. Through the Inquisition-like methods of leading churchmen such as Cardinal Pole and Bishop Bonner, hundreds of people were burnt alive for their faith. In London, Smithfield was the usual place for burnings and a tablet there records that 43 Protestant martyrs suffered there, including John Hallingdale, William Sparrow and Master Gibson. All were bound to the stake with iron chains and surrounded with bundles of wood, which were then lit.

As in the case of Anne Brewen, burning at the stake was reserved for women convicted of murdering their husbands or masters. However, men as well as women could be burned to death on conviction for adultery, incest and bestiality. But until 1789, burning was also the legal punishment for women convicted of treason. In the eighteenth century, treason included the making of false coins. In 1786, twenty thousand people watched the burning of a female counterfeiter at Newgate. Phoebe Harris, a 'well-made little woman', who had forged shillings, was partially hanged before the faggots were lit.

The last recorded instance of death by burning as an execution was in March, 1789, when Christian Murphy, another lady convicted of coining, was put to death. She walked to the stake in the Old Bailey dressed in white 'in token of her innocence'.

The penalty of being boiled alive in water or lead was legal only between 1530 and 1547 and confined to poisoners. One technique was to lower the victim into the bubbling liquid on the end of a chain and then pull him up again and so on until he was scalded to death. In 1530 John Roose, a cook, was boiled to death for throwing poison into a pot of gruel at the house of the Bishop of Rochester, when 17 people were poisoned and two died. A decade later, a woman was boiled for poisoning her mistress and some others.

One of the most barbaric capital punishments to survive for a long time was hanging, drawing and quartering, the legal punishment for treason until 1870. In this punishment which was carried out at a variety of places in London, the victim was first hanged. Then, according to Stow's *Annals*,

> *His body was taken down, his members and bowels cut out and burned in the fire, and his heart taken out by the hangman, who showed it to the people as an arch-traitor's heart; then his head was cut off and his body quartered.*

The pieces of the body were placed in hot pitch for preservation and then exhibited in prominent places such as Temple Bar.

For reasons of modesty, this punishment was never carried out on women.

The Gunpowder Plot conspirators were hanged, drawn and quartered in 1606. Four of them were executed in St. Paul's Churchyard and the other four in Old Palace Yard, Westminster. It was the custom then, for each victim to be dragged through the streets of London from prison to execution site strapped to a hurdle pulled by a horse. There was another custom then, too, which depended on the behaviour of the prisoner. If he impressed the crowd and the authorities by his bravery and conduct (for instance, if he showed true repentance for his crime and loyalty to the monarch), he was permitted to hang until he was dead or certainly unconscious before being cut down and quartered. This privilege was granted to Father Robert Southwell, the Jesuit, in 1595. If, however, the prisoner was unpopular with the spectators and officials, he was cut down from the gallows when still alive (and sometimes conscious) and then mutilated.

> *When the cart was drawn away he was immediately cut down and he stood upon his feet, and struggled with the executioners so that he was holden down by force upon the hurdle for the dismembering.*

In a week during October, 1660, Pepys makes several entries in his diary concerning the Regicides, the men who had signed Charles I's death warrant and who were hanged, drawn and quartered when Charles II came back to England as king.

> 13th. *I went out to Charing Cross to see Major-general Harrison hanged, drawn, and quartered; which was done there, he looking as cheerful as any man could do in that condition. He was presently cut down, and his head and heart shown to the people, at which there was great shouts of joy.*
> 15th. *This morning Mr. Carew was hanged and quartered at Charing Cross; but his quarters, by a great favour, are not to be hanged up.*
> 19th. *This morning Hacker and Axel were hanged and quartered, as the rest are.*
> 20th. *This afternoon . . . I saw the limbs of some of*

our new traytors set upon Aldersgate, which was a sad
sight to see; and a bloody week this and the last have
been, there being ten hanged, drawn, and quartered.

Even Mrs. Pepys was interested in executions. She saw a
particularly gruesome sight at one time, the gibbeting on the
anniversary of the execution of Charles I of the dead bodies of
the Commonwealth leaders Cromwell, Ireton and Bradshaw at
Tyburn, again in revenge. Cromwell had been dead for about
two years. After exposure on London Bridge, their heads were
impaled on an iron-tipped spike on the southern gable of
Westminster Hall. The story goes that Cromwell's head was
blown down in 1686 and hidden by a sentry.

Another popular place for exhibiting heads and sometimes
limbs, was Temple Bar, a gateway of Portland Stone which
marked the limit of the city liberties outside the walls. There
were iron spikes above the centre pediment on which heads
were placed. Spectators could hire spy-glasses to look at them.
Horace Walpole noted in 1746 the heads of the Jacobites
Townley and Fletcher and others displayed at Temple Bar.
Townley's head was removed secretly one night for burial in
the family vault; the others remained until they fell or were
blown down. Heads rotted on Temple Bar until 1776. Temple
Bar itself survived until 1878, serving to cause traffic jams rather
than remind people of the cruel old days.

An execution of especial distaste to the city was that of ex-
Sheriff Henry Cornish in 1685. Cornish, a 'plain, warm, honest
man', was hanged, drawn and quartered in Cheapside within
sight of his home and the Guildhall, charged with high treason
for agreeing to help the cause of the Duke of Monmouth.
Cornish was nothing more than a scapegoat and strengthened
the city's resolve that James II must go.

By the end of the eighteenth century, the full sentence of
hanging, drawing and quartering was reduced to decapitation
after hanging. However, the full sentence was pronounced to
convicted criminals as late as 1812. The wording was barbaric
in any age of London's history:

That you be taken to the place from whence you came,
and from thence be drawn on a hurdle to the place of
execution, where you shall be hanged by the neck, not

*till you are dead; that you be taken down while yet
alive, and your bowels be taken out and burnt before
your face; that your head be then cut off, and your body
cut in four quarters, to be at the King's disposal. And
God Almighty have mercy on your soul.*

When Colonel Edward Despard was hanged for high treason
at Horsemonger Lane Gaol in 1803 and afterwards decapitated,
the authorities took the first part of the sentence literally and
provided a small cart without wheels to drag the Colonel and
six associates, in pairs, across the outer courtyard of the prison
to the stairs leading up to the scaffold. The criminals had their
heads removed by a masked man, said to have been 'a surgeon
of some ability'.

Hanging, drawing and quartering, then, was an imposition
from the past which remained for centuries because of its ability
to cause pain as well as death. Society and the law demanded
this requirement in the punishment for the arch-crime, dis-
loyalty to crown and state. But in the eighteenth century the
military were using a method of killing deserting soldiers that
was both quick and comparatively painless. The method was
death by shooting. The most famous shooting of the century
was that of Admiral Byng, shot in 1757 for cowardice in battle
against the French fleet.

In the previous decade, three soldiers from a Highland
regiment were shot on Tower Green for desertion. Like Byng,
the soldiers were shot 'pour encourager les autres' and to provide
the Government with scapegoats. The three 'Sawnies' were in a
group of one hundred and nine Highlanders who deserted from
their regiment in London when they thought they were going
to be sent to the West Indies. The execution was on July 12th,
1743, in the presence of the other Highland prisoners and a
large escort formed by the Scots Guards.

In the map of London published by John Rocque in 1746, a
small area in Hyde Park just south of Tyburn is marked 'Where
soldiers are shot'. Here deserting soldiers were shot as un-
sparingly as criminals were hanged on the near-by gallows. An
example was one Sergeant Smith who was shot, then hanged.
To earn this punishment, he had deserted to serve with the
French and then had joined the army of Charles Edward, the
Young Pretender.

The largest concentration of shooting in modern times happened during the First World War when eleven German agents were shot in the Tower between 1914 and 1916. The place of execution was near the Martin Tower between the outer and inner walls. One spy was shot in the Tower during the Second World War. He was Josef Jacobs, executed in 1941.

The last hanging followed by beheading in Britain took place in 1820. One hundred and fifty years later, hanging was a crudity of the past.

CHAPTER NINE

PARKS AND SPORTS

The suburbs have gardens, either palled or walled round about very high with their arbours and bowers fit for the purpose. And lest they might be espied in these open places, the proprietesses have their banquetting houses with galleries, turrets and what not else, sumptuously erected, wherein they may, and doubtless do, many of them, play the filthy persons . . .

THE ELIZABETHAN writer, Stubbes, was one of several contemporaries who disapproved of the suburbs to the north of the city where the garden alleys were. These areas thrived for two good reasons: the city itself was too crowded with buildings to contain public parks and large gardens, and the area beyond the walls was out of the jurisdiction of the magistrates. As a result, the open places beyond Bishopsgate and Aldgate were covered with huts, gardens and bowling alleys where disreputable elements gathered.

The daily shifts of these privy houses are masterless men, needy shifters, thieves, cutpurses, unthrifty servants . . . Here may a man pick out mates for all purposes, save such as are good.

From mediaeval times, there were pressures on open spaces surrounding the city. Richer citizens could go far afield to hunt in areas such as Hertfordshire, Middlesex and the Chilterns. But nearer the city, up to the time of the Reformation, London was surrounded by estates belonging to many religious houses. This meant that the youths of the City and Westminster had to go to places such as Smithfield, Tothill Fields, and Moorfields for their sport. Tothill Fields was the centre for young courtiers to practise sport such as archery, fencing, and wrestling. Smithfield, a smaller space, was nearer to the city but had to fulfil a role as a market place as well. The most convenient place for citizens to reach by just walking through Moorgate was Moorfields.

Moorfields was originally a swamp through which the river Walbrook flowed. The citizens found it ideal for throwing rubbish into and the result was that in the winter the swamp was flooded. In the winter, young men went skating on Moorfields with the shin bones of animals lashed to their feet. By the end of the sixteenth century, Moorfields had become hard ground and an Act of Parliament in 1592 prevented the long-leaseholders from enclosing the area. In 1625, the area was properly drained and laid out and the three regular 'fields' became a favourite Sunday gathering place for large crowds of citizens. Said Pepys in June 1661:

> Went to Moorfields, and there walked and stood and saw the wrestling, which I never saw much of before, between the north and west country men.

Moorfields became the model for grounds at Lincoln's Inn and Gray's Inn, which were also laid out with trees and walks.

After the Reformation, the King retained control of large areas around London for hunting purposes and actually fenced in some of it. However restricting this may have seemed at the time, it did mean that much countryside near London was preserved against building and many spaces became popular parks before long. London's most important park, Hyde Park, was open to the public in mid-seventeenth century. Citizens then were fortunate to have places to 'let off steam' by riding, horse-racing, tennis, pall mall (the forerunner of croquet), and duelling.

If it was not difficult for Londoners to take part in active sports, neither was it hard for them to set aside small areas outside the city walls for spectator sports and fairs. The most famous sports-show and fair of them all was Bartholomew Fair at Smithfield. The origins of the Fair are believed to go back to 1123, when a prebendary from St. Paul's, Rahere, founded the Augustin priory and London's first hospital at Smithfield. The priory was suppressed in 1545 but the hospital was retained. Rahere may have been the founder of the Fair which was held annually at Smithfield for a fortnight from the saint's day on August 24th. The Fair was once important as a cloth fair, but by 1591 had become famous as an annual carnival featuring puppet shows, monster rarities, fortune tellers, sideshows, wrestling, boxing, and horse and cattle dealing. Everyone who was anyone came to the Fair, including the Lord Mayor and Aldermen. However, pickpockets came too, as a German visitor related at this time:

> *While we were at the show, one of our company, Tobias Salander, doctor of physic, had his pocket picked of his purse with nine crowns which without doubt was so cleverly taken from him . . . that the doctor did not in the least perceive it.*

The Fair was threatened with violence in the summer of 1589 when 500 discharged soldiers drifted up to London after returning from Portugal with the unsuccessful expedition led by Norris and Drake. With an attack imminent on the Fair, martial law was proclaimed and two thousand militia men were called out. A proclamation threatened all mariners, soldiers and masterless men (with summary execution) if they did not procure warrants to their homes within two days. It was at least six months before the panic died down. Where force had failed to close the Fair, disease succeeded. Plague in 1593, 1598 and 1665 caused the city authorities to forbid the holding of the Fair in those years. An Elizabethan proclamation commanded that

> *. . . All manner of persons, of whatsoever estate, degree, or condition they be, having recourse to this Fair, keep the peace.*

However, as the years went by, the Fair grew more and more disreputable. It lingered on until it was finally closed in 1855.

A shorter-lived fair, and one with a wide reputation for attracting the dregs of London was the May Fair. This annual event was held from the reign of Edward I up to its final abolition in 1760. Every now and then the Fair's suppression was ordered. This happened in 1702, but when the constables arrived to close it, a vicious battle broke out between them and a crowd of soldiers and prizefighters. One constable was killed. The magistrates bowed to this show of public opinion and allowed the Fair to continue, despite the 'drunkeness, fornication, gaming and lewdness' it provoked. Southwark's Our Lady Fair had much the same reputation and it, too, had to finish in 1763.

The Southwark area of Bankside was a holiday place for London crowds over many centuries and it was here that the cruel amusements of bull-baiting and bear-baiting were enjoyed away from the interference of the city authorities. The bear-gardens were in the open space behind the houses lining the waterside. A favourite approach from the river led up Paris Garden Stairs opposite the west end of St. Paul's. There were at least two gardens, built in the shape of small amphitheatres. The bulls were tethered and then worried by bull-dogs who tried to kill them by seizing them by the throat. A fresh bull would be produced if any bulls in the ring became wounded or tired. This would sometimes be followed by the entertainment of whipping a blinded bear. Five or six men would carry this out with whips, safe from the bear who would be tethered by a chain. The bear, however, would lash out and occasionally throw down one of his tormentors. In 1623, the Spanish Ambassador was shown a spectacle which consisted of turning a white bear into the Thames and setting swimming dogs to bait it. Bull and bear-baiting were not abolished until 1835.

Mr. Pepys went to Bankside several times to see bull-baiting and once he was nearly involved in a dangerous riot after a prize-fight:

> *Abroad, and stopped at Bear-garden stairs, there to see a prize fought. But the house so full there was no getting in there, so forced to go through an alehouse into the pit, where the bears are baited; and upon a stool did see them fight, which they did very furiously, a butcher and a waterman. The former had the better all along till by and by the latter dropped his sword out of his hand, and the butcher, whether not seeing his sword dropped I know not, but did give him a cut*

> *over the wrist, so as he was disabled to fight any*
> *longer. But Lord! to see how in a minute the whole*
> *stage was full of watermen to revenge the foul play,*
> *and the butchers to defend their fellow, though most*
> *blamed him; and there they all fell to it to knocking*
> *down and cutting many on each side. It was pleasant*
> *to see, but that I stood in the pit, and feared that in the*
> *tumult I might get some hurt. At last the natter broke*
> *up, and so I away.*

In the next century, another place became popular for offering the same amusements as Bankside. This was Hockley-in-the-Hole, north of Clerkenwell Road, where both nobility and riff-raff could watch bull-baiting, bear-bating, sword-matches, wrestling, cudgelling, cock-fighting, dog-fighting and boxing-matches between women. A match in the last category was fought in 1772 between Elizabeth Wilkinson and Hannah Highfield. However undignified the contest must have appeared, the challenge and acceptance were correctly formal.

> *I, Elizabeth Wilkinson of Clerkenwell, having some*
> *words with Hannah Highfield, and requiring satisfac-*
> *tion, do invite her to meet me on the stage and box for*
> *three guineas, each woman holding half a crown in*
> *each hand, and the first woman that drops her money*
> *to lose the battle.*
> *I, Hannah Highfield, of Newgate Market, hearing of*
> *the resoluteness of Elizabeth Wilkinson, will not fail,*
> *God willing, to give her more blows than words, desiring*
> *home blows, and of her no favour.*

The reason why each woman held a coin in each hand was to prevent scratching. Another place to see female fighters was at Mr. Stokes's Amphitheatre in Islington Road where prize-fights were staged. The most renowned lady boxer of the time was 'Bruising Peg', who defeated an opponent in 1768 'in a terrible manner'.

Freak shows never failed to attract Londoners, who could see them everywhere. In the eighteenth century you could see a man who 'could twist his hip bone up to his shoulder blade'; a seven-foot-tall eighteen-year-old girl, who would parade for your family by appointment; a fourteen-foot-long pig; and a 'real Wild Man of the Woods'.

This example appeared at Bartholomew Fair in 1667:

> The Wonder of Nature
> *Girl, above Sixteen Years of Age, born in Cheshire,*
> *and not above Eighteen inches long, having shed the*
> *Teeth seven several Times, and not a perfect Bone in*
> *any part of her, only the Head; yet she hath all her*
> *senses to Admiration, and Discourses, Reads very well,*
> *Sings, Whistles, and all very pleasant to hear. God*
> *Save the King.*

For more cultured citizens, the appearance of coffee houses at the time of the Restoration provided welcome facilities. Coffee-houses sold alcohol as well as coffee but people went to them not so much to drink as to read newspapers, discuss politics and listen to debates. Different professions and trades had their favourite coffee houses. From these meeting places, the first London clubs grew. But coffee houses were never completely tranquil; many duels and brawls started in their seemingly calm environment.

Another source of entertainment which gave Londoners much pleasure and allowed them to express their feelings were the theatres. Theatres in England started in London, derived from churches and churchyards where miracle and morality plays were performed. But the theatres originated outside the city; the authorities feared the spread of plague among the audiences, accidents in the theatres, and moral danger to the young. So players had to be licensed and the plays read by Aldermen before their performance. As a result, the plays and the players went to Shoreditch and Bankside, outside the reach of authority, and sixteenth-century Londoners could then patronise theatres such as the 'Theatre' at Shoreditch and the 'Rose' at Bankside.

The audiences were unruly, to say the least. Apart from eating and drinking during performances, smoking and spitting, they would make an uproar if they disliked what they saw and confirm their disapproval with rotten eggs. In Boswell's time, no one queued at theatres. So when the doors opened, people could be seriously hurt in the rush for the benches. Theatre managers used to reduce the price of admittance half-way through the final act. As a result, many people came then, and so there was a custom of presenting a one-act entertainment for this second audience. In January, 1763, there was an attempt to abolish this custom of second price. The audiences responded by destroying the benches and smashing the chandeliers. However, the actors had some protection from the audience. A row of sharp spikes separated theatregoers from the musicians in the orchestra.

There was also the danger of fire in early theatres as the lights were candles placed around the theatre, even on stage. The same boisterousness followed audiences into the next century who cheered, booed, and fought as they pleased. Another profession operated in large numbers in theatreland as well; that of prostitution which made London infamous in the late Victorian age. But there was no decrease in the popularity of the stage. London in the reign of Edward VII supported twelve music halls and thirty-three theatres in the centre of the city, and twenty-five music halls and twenty-two theatres in the suburbs.

For all ages and all sexes, however, the best universal free entertainment were the open spaces in and around London. In the seventeenth century, Londoners could enjoy more than Hyde Park, Moorfields, Gray's Inn and Lincoln's Inn. There was Spring Gardens, near what is now Trafalgar Square; St. James's Park, originally a swampy meadow and improved by Charles II; and nearer the City, Totnam Court, Lamb's Conduit and Bednal Green.

But the parks contained more than rustic charm. There were riding accidents, such as befell Cromwell in Hyde Park, according to Carlyle:

> *The horses, beautiful animals, tasting of the whip, became unruly; galloped would not be checked, but took to plunging; plunged the postillion down; plunged or shook his Highness down, dragging him by the foot for some time so that 'a pistol went off in his pocket', to the amazement of men. Whereupon? Whereupon— his Highness got up again, little the worse . . .*

There were soldiers, engaged in military training. There were duels (see Chapter 10); for instance, Viscount Ligonier v Count Vittoria Alfieri in Upper St. James's Park (this became Green

Park), 1771, and Lord Mohun (the same man who had been tried for murder—twice) v the 4th Duke of Hamilton in Hyde Park, 1712. In the former duel, both men were wounded and Ligonier was able to return to a theatre to watch the last act, but in the latter encounter, the two men killed each other.

Hyde Park also had highwaymen. When Horace Walpole was robbed there by James M'Lean, his face was blackened with powder and shot marks when M'Lean's pistol exploded close to him. For some time, a bell was rung at intervals to assemble people wishing to cross the Park to go to town without being robbed. Another unpleasant aspect of London's countryside at the time was that many of the fields ringing the city consisted of rubbish dumps and manure heaps.

Regent's Park was once known as Marylebone Park Fields and did not become a park until 1838. The large lake there was the scene of a disaster in the winter of 1866–7. Over two hundred skaters fell into the lake when the ice gave way and nearly forty of them were drowned.

In the eighteenth century, St. James's Park was locked at night and left unguarded and unlit. However, 6,500 people had keys issued by authority and the dark park was 'the scene of a good deal of business in a wicked way'. Boswell met many ladies of the streets in St. James's Park.

Parks of a smaller kind and ancestors of amusement parks were the tea-gardens which were extremely popular during the eighteenth century. Most tea-gardens were some way out of town as can be gleaned from their names which included Marybone Gardens, Belsize House, Sadler's Wells and Hampstead Wells. They provided refreshment and mild sport, befitting anyone who had walked all the way from town. Marybone Gardens was encircled by a brick wall set with fruit trees and had a circular walk six paces wide and 485 paces round 'double set with quick-set hedges kept in excellent order, and indented like town walls'. In the centre was a bowling green 'much used by persons of quality'. Tea-garden patrons could also play trap-ball (an early form of cricket), real tennis, and skittles.

The two most famous gardens were Vauxhall Gardens and Ranelagh. Vauxhall was derived from Foxhall, in its turn the common name for Falk's Hall. In 1610, the riverside had not yet been laid out in pleasure gardens, but the place was already a common resort for thieves and vagabonds. In 1728, Jonathan Tyers took a lease of New Spring Gardens (they were situated just north of the present Vauxhall Bridge) and reconstructed them and improved them. Vauxhall Gardens was then opened to the public in 1732. Admission was one guinea, the hours 9 p.m. to 4 a.m. There were a pavilion, tree-lined walks and a semicircular arcade. Horace Walpole went with a party in 1750 and ate minced chicken, strawberries and cherries in a private booth. He noted the fountains and nightingales, 'the best band of music in England', and the thousand lamps . . .

> . . . so disposed that they all take fire together, almost as quick as lightening, and dart such a sudden blaze as is perfectly surprising.

In the nineteenth century, rope-dancing, fortune-telling and balloons became attractions, but the rowdies were moving in again and the Gardens were closed in 1859.

The attractions of Ranelagh were shorter-lived than those of Vauxhall, even though many diaries and letters of the period refer to them. Ranelagh was opened in 1742 with the feature of the famous Rotunda, a building 150 feet in diameter with a central fireplace, a double row of gaily-painted boxes and a circle of glittering chandeliers. Visitors enjoyed entertainments such as masquerades, fireworks, dancing and concerts. In Smollett's *Humphrey Clinker*, a young girl gives her impressions of Ranelagh:

> Ranelagh looks like the enchanted palace of a genius, adorned with the most exquisite performances of painting, carving, and gilding, enlightened with a thousand golden lamps, that emulate the noon-day sun; crowded with the great, the rich, the gay, the happy, and the fair . . .

If any of the great, rich, gay, happy and fair were young men of good health, they had to be on the alert for the army's press-gang who toured the Gardens regularly searching for likely candidates.

For all Ranelagh's glitter, its end came sooner than that of Vauxhall. The gardens were closed in 1803 and the Rotunda demolished in 1805. Society had grown tired of jostling with the 'motley swarm'. The gardens are now part of the grounds of the Royal Hospital, Chelsea. They blaze with colour once a year at the time of the Chelsea Flower Show.

Other pleasure gardens were closing down, too. Cuper's Gardens, opened in 1691 opposite Hungerford Stairs, closed because of the 'profligacy of the company by whom it was frequented'. The owner of the Temple of Flora, near Westminster Bridge, was gaoled in 1796 for running a disorderly house. One last attempt to maintain a successful garden was made in 1843 when Cremorne was opened in Chelsea. But like the other gardens, it lost its patrons when it became rowdy and disreputable. Cremorne closed in 1877.

A sport which was followed with enthusiasm from the twelfth century up to modern times was cock-fighting. In Fitz-Stephen's description of London there is a chapter on Sports and Pastimes which starts with children's sports. Every year on Shrove Tuesday

> . . . *the schoolboys do bring cocks of the game to their master, and all the forenoon they delight themselves in cock-fighting.*

But the first building erected specifically for cock-fighting was added to Whitehall Palace by Henry VIII. A second building close to this one is mentioned by Pepys, who himself went to a cockpit in Shoe Lane:

> December 21st, 1663. *To Shoe Lane to see a cocke-fighting at a new pit there, a spot I was never at in my life: but Lord! to see the strange variety of people, from Parliament-man to the poorest 'prentices, bakers, brewers, butchers, draymen, and what not; and all these fellows one with another cursing and betting. I soon had enough of it. It is strange to see how people of this poor rank, that look as if they had not bread to put in their mouths, shall bet three or four pounds at a time, and lose it, and yet bet as much the next battle, so that one of them will lose ten or twenty pounds at a meeting.*

Perhaps Pepys would have felt at home in a modern betting shop. In the reign of Queen Anne, a new pit was built near Gray's Inn and another building replaced the Whitehall pit. This was the Royal Cockpit, Birdcage Walk. During the eighteenth century, cock-fighting became what amounted to a national craze. There were fights between villages. There were contests between counties. The champions of Somerset and Wiltshire fought each other for two days. Sometimes battles were arranged with sixteen cocks to a side. The fight went on until one cock was left alive. There was a cruel variation: cock-throwing, in which sticks were thrown at a tethered cockerel until the bird died. Among the places where cock-fighting could be seen were Hockley-in-the-Hole, Clerkenwell; Jewin Street, Cripplegate; and Tufton Street, Westminster, which was there in 1821. James Boswell spent five hours at the Royal Cockpit:

> *I then went to the Cockpit, which is a circular room in the middle of which the cocks fight. It is seated round with rows gradually rising. The pit and the seats are all covered with mat. The cocks, nicely cut and dressed and armed with silver heels, are set down and fight with amazing bitterness and resolution. Some of them were quickly dispatched. One pair fought three quarters of an hour. The uproar and noise of betting is prodigious. A great deal of money made a very quick circulation from hand to hand. There was a number of professed gamblers there . . . I was shocked to see the distraction and anxiety of the betters. I was sorry for the poor cocks. I looked around to see if any of the spectators pitied them when mangled and torn in a most cruel manner, but I could not observe the smallest sign in any countenance. I was therefore not ill pleased to see them endure mental torment.**

Cock-fighting was made illegal, even on private premises, in 1849. After that date, any cock-fighting which was continued tended to be followed surreptitiously in the country among farmers and gentry. Ban apart, no reasons have been put forward why such a popular and easily-organised sport should

---

* *Boswell's London Journal* edited F. A. Pottle (Heinemann).

have declined so rapidly during the first half of the nineteenth century.

A sport which lasted longer than cock-fighting, even though it was not so popular, was dog-fighting. This was probably because dogs were more expensive to train and maintain. In Victorian times, dogs of the bull breed were brought to fighting trim as if they were prize-fighters—which, in a way, they were. Bets would be made on the outcome of the fight, which could take place almost anywhere scheduled. As a substitute for cock-fighting, ratting appears to have been popular among the lower classes. Dogs of all kinds could be used to catch rats in pits attached to public houses. Bets were laid according to the weight of the dog and the number of rats expected to be caught within an agreed time. Small bull dogs and terriers were used, and often the animals would be covered with scars from rat bites.

The last of the old human prize-fights took place in the second half of the century. For years, prize-fighting had been associated with the underworld. The sight of men fighting with bare knuckles until one was totally exhausted, 'deaf and blind with blood and contusions, his broken hands and wrists swollen like sponges, half moribund with shock and fatigue' appealed to audiences of the lowest repute. The last prize-fight to arouse any national interest took place in 1860.

Horse-racing nearly went the same way as prize-fighting. But this sport had more powerful patrons who were able eventually to put pressures on to the management of horses and on the control of betting. As the popularity of horse-racing grew, so did it attract the money of the Londoner who wanted the excitement of a sporting gamble.

A concern for the welfare of animals, just as much as of humans, helped to speed the end of the bloodiest sports which took place in public. And when the era of the team game began with football and cricket, the desire for 'fair play' curtailed much exuberance in park and arena, theatre and club.

CHAPTER TEN

SWORD AND PISTOL

Tweedledum and Tweedledee
Agreed to have a battle.

MEN HAVE always quarrelled and fought each other on the smallest excuse ranging from bravado to the settlement of an affair of honour. But the practice of duelling, as a fair means of settling a quarrel instead of, say, assassination or ambush, did not become popular in London until the seventeenth century. In the comparatively short time that duelling flourished up to the middle of the nineteenth century there were many dramatic and unnecessary deaths. Authority, though officially against the practice, found that many exponents of duelling came from high ranks of society.

For example, one of the first duels of honour to be fought in Britain took place in 1609 in Islington between Sir George Wharton and Sir James Stewart. Sir George was the son of Lord Wharton, Sir James was the godson of King James I; both were favourites at court. However, each killed the other in the duel and on the order of the king, both were buried in one grave. James I showed his disapproval of the rising popularity of duelling in his *Proclamation against Private Challenges and Combats* published four years later. However, there was no prosecution of the Earl of Dorset when he killed Lord Bruce in a duel during the same year.

During the Civil War, the nobility forgot individual quarrels and united together in the struggle against the Parliamentarians. Duelling became an irrelevant part of etiquette when men were dying in battle. But during the Protectorate, there was enough duelling to provoke an ordinance which not only prohibited duelling but also stated that death by duelling was to be regarded as murder. With the restoration, duelling returned to high status and young bloods settled quarrels with the sword in parks and public walks. Many disputes were started in fashionable taverns, the revived theatres and in the new coffee houses, and not all of them were between two men, as Mr. Pepys recorded in 1668. Each protagonist had two seconds who fought with him:

> *Much discourse of the duel yesterday between the Duke of Buckingham, Holmes, and one Jenkins, on one side, and my Lord of Shrewsbury, Sir John Talbot, and one Bernerd Howard, on the other side: and all about my Lady Shrewsbury, who is at this time, and hath for a great while been, a mistress to the Duke of Buckingham. And so her husband challenged him, and they met yesterday in a close near Barne-Elmes and there fought: and my Lord Shrewsbury is run through the body from the right breast through the shoulder; and Sir John Talbot all along up one of his arms; and Jenkins killed upon the place, and the rest all in a little measure wounded.*

But there was much more discourse in 1719 at the time of the famous duel between Lord Mohun and the Duke of Hamilton in Hyde Park. As a result of this duel, an attempt was made to introduce a bill into the House of Commons to suppress duelling. The bill was rejected, but the public attitude to duelling had now sharpened, in view of the events which ended in the death of the Duke, a 'frank, honest, and good natured man'. Why the Duke and Mohun fought is not clear but the two men met at seven one morning in Hyde Park. The two seconds fought each other as well. The Duke's second was Colonel Hamilton of the Foot Guards and a Mr. George MacCartney acted for Lord Mohun. According to Swift:

> *The dog Mohun was killed on the spot, but while the Duke was over him, Mohun shortened his sword, and stabbed him in the shoulder to the heart. The Duke*

*was helped towards the lake-house, by the ring . . . and
died on the grass.*

The wives of the two duellists reacted very differently to the
event. The Duchess was still asleep when her husband's body
was brought home in the family coach at eight. Swift wrote,
when referring to her grief: 'she has moved my very soul'.
Lady Mohun, however, complained that her husband's body
should not have been placed on her best bed as it spoiled the
bedclothes.

While this duel was the most notable among many others
fought in Hyde Park, there were others involving famous names
such as the future Earl of Bath who fought Lord Hervey in
1731 in what is now Green Park, and Lord Byron, great-uncle
of the poet, who fought his neighbour, Mr. Chaworth, in 1765
in Pall Mall. In the former duel, the combatants were parted
after each had been slightly wounded. In the latter duel, Lord
Byron had to stand trial in the House of Lords for murder.
By this time, duellists had to be prepared to answer for their
actions in a court of law. Lord Byron's fellow peers found him
not guilty of murder but guilty of manslaughter, which meant
that he was set free immediately. The form of duelling was
changing, too. Pistols were now regarded as fairer weapons for
duelling as the opponents could be kept apart during their
contest.

The etiquette followed in duelling was simple. A man who
considered himself dishonoured felt that his honour could only
be restored by fighting the man who had dishonoured him. He
would therefore challenge his opponent, either personally, or
through his seconds, who were usually two of his friends. The
opponent would appoint two seconds as well, and between
them, all the seconds would agree about the rules to be
followed in the duel. The challenged men had the privilege of
choosing the weapons. In the case of a small insult, a slight
wound or an exchange of shots might be enough to satisfy
honour. But if the insult was a serious one, the two principals
might fight until one of the principals was seriously wounded or
killed—*à outrance*. A surgeon usually attended to give aid
where needed.

Duels fought with swords required a piece of level ground
where the combatants could move up and down freely. When

pistols were used, spots were marked by the seconds on the ground at an agreed distance apart, which was usually eight to twelve yards. The duellists would stand on these markers and fire at each other on an agreed signal given by a second. Sometimes, on agreement, the protagonists would fire at each other at their own discretion.

In George III's reign, 172 duels were reported in which 91 people were killed. One of the most well-known duels and one of the earliest to take place with pistols was that between John Wilkes and Lord Talbot in 1762. Neither was hurt and they parted good friends. Later, more famous names were involved in duelling. They included:

Richard Brinsley Sheridan v Major Thomas Matthews 1772

William Adam v Charles James Fox 1779

William Pitt v George Tierney 1796

Lord Castlereagh v George Canning 1809

At the beginning of the nineteenth century, there were many duels which involved soldiers and sailors. Two in 1803, one in Hyde Park, the other near Primrose Hill, resulted in three dead officers and a naval officer going on trial for murder. The captain, one Macnamara, was acquitted, but many a young buck was shaken when an army major was hanged for murder in 1808 when he killed a brother officer in a duel. Britain's most famous soldier of the day fought as a duellist in Battersea Park in 1829; he was the Duke of Wellington and his opponent was the Earl of Winchelsea. This duel was regarded with amazement by the general public. The Duke had been roused by a letter written by the Earl who attacked the Duke's patronage of the establishment of King's College, London. To fight a duel over such a trivial matter seemed absurd, particularly when the challenger was so eminent a man.

Charles Greville takes up the story in his memoirs:

They met at Wimbledon at eight o'clock. There were many people about, who saw what passed. They stood at a distance of fifteen paces. Before they began Hardinge went up to Lords Winchelsea and Falmouth, and said he must protest against the proceeding, and declare that their conduct in refusing an apology when Lord Winchelsea was so much in the wrong filled him with disgust. The Duke fired and missed, and then Winchelsea fired in the air. He immediately pulled out of his pocket the paper which has since appeared, but in which the word 'apology' was omitted. The Duke read it and said it would not do. Lord Falmouth said he was not come there to quibble about words, and that he was ready to make the apology in whatever terms would be satisfactory, and the word 'apology' was inserted on the ground. The Duke then touched his hat, said 'Good morning, my Lords', mounted his horse, and rode off.

Soldiers, however, hastened the end of duelling. The Earl of Cardigan fought a much-publicised duel on Wimbledon Common in 1840 which ended when his opponent, Captain Tuckett, was wounded. Cardigan was tried by the House of Lords and acquitted to general disapproval of the public. But there was a public outcry when Lieutenant-Colonel David Fawcett was killed by his brother-in-law in a duel in 1843. The result was that the War Office took steps to make duelling a court-martial offence with cashiering as a penalty. From then on, the duel of honour belonged to the past.

Duelling has only a small part in London's history but it took many of the characteristics of street fighting into the peace of the parks. It was on one hand something which took place privately, albeit in a public place, yet on the other, because it was exercised by leading members of society, it helped to encourage young men to prove their courage in bloody contest. To that extent, duelling deserves a mention as part of *Evil London*.

CHAPTER ELEVEN

MACABRE AND MULTIFARIOUS

*The heyday of condemned murderers in Tussauds was
that unnatural time when executions were no longer
public shows, between 1868—when the hangman
Calcroft officiated in public for the last time, and 1965
—when capital punishment was abolished. During this
period an execution was like a wedding without a
feast; an official pronounced the words and the rest
took place behind bolted doors. The criminal died
without the possibility of sympathy and encouragement
from the populace, the hangman did his task without
the check of an audience and the public was left with
the wildest imaginings about what took place. No
wonder the Chamber of Horrors became a place of
popular resort.*

THIS PARAGRAPH comes from a souvenir leaflet issued by
Madame Tussaud's Exhibition in the Marylebone Road. When
Madame Tussaud arrived in England in 1802, bringing models
of the heads of many victims of the guillotine, she was able to
win fame and fortune by showing these and other realistic wax
portraits. For Londoners of the time, exhibitions such as
Madame Tussaud's carried out much the same sort of function
as films do today; they froze history. If the figures were macabre
or horrific, so much the better from the viewing public's point
of view. And this was in an age, up to 1867, when people of all

ages and sexes could watch executions.

London has had a variety of museums and exhibitions. Many of the cultural type are established British institutions; those related to show-business have passed away. A typical museum in the latter category was Rackstraw's in Fleet Street. Here, viewers could see figures of Coan, the Norfolk dwarf and Bamford, the giant. Bamford was 7 ft. 4 in. tall and on his death, £200 was offered for his body for dissection. There were also bones of beasts and fish, including the skeleton of a whale more than 70 feet long. Rackstraw's Museum was open from 1736 to 1772.

Another museum and one where Victorians could see living exhibits was Bullock's. This was set up in the Egyptian Hall, Piccadilly, in 1812 and from time to time housed such curiosities as the Living Skeleton, a man 5 ft. 7½ in. in height and weighing only 5½ stones; Tom Thumb, the well-known midget; and the sensational Siamese Twins.

One institution which still contains 'a large collection of specimens of morbid anatomy' is the Royal College of Surgeons, Lincoln's Inn Fields. The college was founded in 1745 and after the Act of 1752 received the bodies of dead murderers for dissection as part of their sentences. The first hall of the college was conveniently placed (particularly after 1783, when the place of execution was transferred to Newgate from Tyburn) in the Old Bailey. In 1809, the college moved to Lincoln's Inn Fields. One famous body to come to the college for dissection after hanging was that of Earl Ferrers in 1760. Another belonged to Elizabeth Brownrigg, hanged in 1767 for flogging a female apprentice to death. A story is told how in 1803 the body of an executed criminal had an electric current passed through it. One of the twitching limbs struck one of the experimenters who died of the shock. The museum can only be visited through the introduction of a member. Among its exhibits are the skeletons of Jonathan Wild; Charles Byrne, a 7 ft. 8 in. tall Irish giant; and a 20 in. high dwarf, aged 10.

Some unusual effigies, Tussaud-style, which also relate to dead people are the wax figures in the museum in the Norman undercroft of Westminster Abbey. William Gaunt commented:

While the great sculptured tombs impress us as works
of art, the Abbey contains a collection of images at

the same time more lifelike and more macabre, which
constitutes one of its most fascinating and perhaps
*least-known features.**

These figures are illustrative of a time when wax figures were
made of royal personages and famous people after their deaths
to be used in their funerals. The effigies were carried in procession or placed on the coffins. Later, the effigies were used as
standby memorials on tombs while the permanent sculpture
was being prepared. The figures were generally life-sized and
the features were often modelled from a death mask. Among
those on show are Elizabeth I, Queen Anne, Charles II, William
Pitt and Lord Nelson. All are in contemporary costume dressed
as they would have been in real life. Lord Nelson's effigy was
made after his burial in St. Paul's, in order to attract people
back to Westminster Abbey. Madame Tussaud was once asked
to help mend the collection. Indignant, she told the Dean of
Westminster: 'See you Sare, I have a shop of mine own to
look after, and I do not look after other people's shops.'

A hawker of broadsheets gave Henry Mayhew a brief and
snide glimpse of Madame Tussaud in action when he was
evaluating the popularity of murderers in terms of sales:

> *Daniel Good, though, was a first-rater; and would have*
> *been much better if it hadn't been for that there*
> *Madame Toosow. You see, she went down to Roe-*
> *hampton, and guv 2£ for the werry clogs as he used to*
> *wash his master's carriage in; so, in course, when the*
> *harristocracy could go and see the real things—the*
> *werry identical clogs—in the Chamber of 'Orrors, why*
> *the people wouldn't look at our authentic portraits of*
> *the fiend in human form.*

The Tussaud 'shop,' opened in Baker Street in 1835, always
had a Separate Room to show its more gruesome exhibits. From
1844, the room was called the Chamber of Horrors. The greater
number of its figures are executed murderers, many of whom
have been mentioned in this book. However, there are also some
respectable policemen and hangmen, together with victims,
regicides and eccentrics. The chamber's links are very much

---

* *London* by **William Gaunt (Batsford).**

with the past; the impact of seeing a murderer, or rather his image, who captured popular attention by his deed and his fate some years ago, has lessened. But Tussauds rightly recall Guy Thorne's observations, written in *The Drunkard* at the beginning of the century:

> *It is not a place, that artists and imaginative people can enter in and easily forget. Row upon row of faces which differ in every way from one to another, and yet are dreadfully alike. For these great sinister dolls, so unreal and so real, have all a likeness. The smirk of cruelty and cunning seems to lie upon their waxen masks. Colder than life, far colder than death, they give forth emanations which strike the very heart with woe and desolation.*

This collective impression given by figures including those of Crippen, Sheppard, Haigh, Lord George Gordon, Heath and Christie helps to invoke an image of a London as a city with dark, dangerous corners, where sudden and violent death could emerge without warning.

While the deeds of the villains in the Chamber of Horrors have effected individuals, events which affected the lives of all Londoners in two world wars are recorded in the Imperial War Museum, Lambeth. The London of the Blitz, the air raid shelter, the rubble-strewn streets is recorded here with relics and art. This was the time when death came not furtively from around the corner but exploded from the skies.

Twentieth-century London has a big advantage over London of the past. Film and sound recordings can capture every significant event. Furthermore, mass media ensure that no events affecting this history can be hidden for long. London, with angel's halo or devil's fork, has to function in public and this can only be to the advantage of its citizens and of the country.

Museum, book, newspaper or film; all media help to bear out Ruskin's contention in *Stones of Venice*:

> *Multitudes think they like to do evil; yet no man ever really enjoyed doing evil since God made the world.*

CHAPTER TWELVE

BAWDS AND BROTHELS

No stew-holder to receive any woman of religion, or any man's wife.
No single woman to take money to lie with any man, but she lie with him all night till the morrow.
No man to be drawn or enticed into any stew-house.
The constables, bailiffs, and others, every week to search every stew-house.

THESE CLAUSES are from an Act of 1162 which granted a royal licence to the stews of Bankside. This area was packed with brothels and staffed, 'since English people disdain to be bawds', with women from Flanders. These ladies were known as 'Flanders Mares' and later, as 'Winchester Geese', because many of the stews were in the Liberty of the Clink under the juris-diction of the Bishop of Winchester. The area became even more unsavoury in the fourteenth century when there was a large exodus from the City of the underworld who crossed the Thames to Southwark to avoid the influence of the magistrates. How-ever, some order prevailed among the brothels. Not only were there regulations but also brothels could be immediately recognised. According to Stow, they had:

> . . . *signs on their fronts, towards the Thames, not hanged out but painted on the walls, as a Boar's head, the Cross keys, the Gun, the Castle, the Crane, the Cardinal's hat, the Bell, the Swan, etc.*

Officialdom invested in brothels, as did, for instance, William Walworth, the Lord Mayor who killed Wat Tyler. Previously, Tyler and his rebels had destroyed several of Walworth's stews as they marched into London, so the Lord Mayor may have had this in mind when he struck Tyler. Another reason why brothels boomed was that social and religious pressures demanded that marriages should not be dissolved. But when Henry VIII disestablished the Church and withdrew the royal licence from the Southwark stews, they continued, popular as ever, as one of London's major brothel areas, well into the eighteenth century.

In the fourteenth century, the Smithfield district was also enjoying some fame as a bawdy-house area, with a considerable number of brothels. One street is still with us from those days— Cock Lane. In 1420, the classic name of a 'common bawd' was entered in the Calendar Rolls. She was Joan Jolybody. Visitors to Elizabethan brothels would probably refer to the 'wapping morts' they met in 'trugging houses'. If they were near Newgate, they probably went to the Turnmill Street district near which was the notorious Picthatch bawdy house. But even the road to Westminster, the Strand, contained lodging houses which held women who 'ambushed' men travelling between court and city.

However much authority turned a blind eye to prostitution, there were times when the law struck, as it did in 1598, according to the Middlesex Session Rolls:

> *Elizabeth Holland, being found guilty at the sessions of keeping a brothel at Pickthatch, the court adjudged that she shall be put into a cart at Newgate and be carted with a paper on her head showing her offence, and from thence to Smithfield, from thence to her house, thence to the Standard in Cheapside, and thence to Bridewell where she shall be punished; and all the way basins to be rung before her. Thence she shall be taken to Newgate, and there to remain until she have paid a fine of £40.*

While the Puritans made great efforts to close entertainments such as theatres and pleasure-gardens, they surprisingly allowed the brothels to remain open. In addition to Bankside and Smithfield, colonies of night-houses could be found in Drury

Lane, Catherine Street off the Strand, Shoe Lane, Cowcross Street, Whitecross Street, Kent Street in Southwark and Ratcliff Highway. All these names can be found in London today with the exception of Ratcliff Highway, which is now called, plainly, the Highway. After the Restoration, when rich and poor relaxed after the restrictions of the Commonwealth, other areas came into prominence as places for dubious assignations. For instance, Covent Garden Church was a well-known hunting ground for wives who wanted lovers and for husbands who sought mistresses. For those with less expensive tastes, prostitutes could now be visited at Whetstone Park, between Holborn and Lincoln's Inn. Some of the new coffee houses had brothels attached and the best head-dressers' shops had prostitutes available for 'about a guinea purchase'. Coffee houses offering these special services placed a sign outside showing a woman's arm and hand holding the coffee-pot.

In the eighteenth century, a 'Who's Who' of courtesans sold out every time a new edition was published. This was *Henry's List of Covent Garden Ladies*. This work was published under a variety of titles. A French visitor commented:

> . . . *This list, which is very numerous, points out their places of abode, and gives the most circumstantial and exact detail of their features, their stature and the several qualifications for which they are remarkable.*

It was not difficult to find prostitutes. They were not only in bawdy houses and bagnios but also in the streets, theatres and pleasure gardens. Droves would appear in the evening, soliciting every male passer-by. Most prostitutes took their clients to rooms, but weather permitting, were available in parks or secluded corners of streets. According to James Boswell who had many sexual adventures in London in 1762–63, there was a choice of lady ranging

> . . . *from the splendid Madam at fifty guineas a night, down to the civil nymph with white-thread stockings who tramps along the Strand and will resign her engaging person to your honour for a pint of wine and a shilling.**

---

* *Boswell's London Journal* edited F. A. Pottle (Heinemann).

In fact, several of Boswell's encounters were in the Strand. Otherwise, he went to St. James's Park to find women. Once he found a 'fresh, agreeable young girl' in Downing Street, where he had lodgings. On another occasion Boswell enjoyed a girl on Westminster Bridge. He also visited the Shakespeare's Head tavern with two girls and 'solaced my existence with them, one after another, according to their seniority'. Other well-known taverns frequented by prostitutes at the time were Wetherby's, Marjoram's, Malby's and the Rose, all near Covent Garden. Some of the girls were only thirteen or fourteen. For men who wanted something completely different, there was the White Swan for homosexuals and a brothel staffed entirely by negresses.

At the beginning of the nineteenth century, prostitution in London was a wide and expanding profession. Estimates of the number of prostitutes varied between 50,000 and 80,000. By the 1850's, the profession was openly conducted in nearly three thousand brothels and in parks, passages and lodgings all over the city. Many women were forced to become prostitutes on a full-time or part-time basis because of necessity; wages were low and society had low regard for any woman who had fallen. The tendency for Victorian middle-class men to marry late in life meant that prostitution supplied a paradoxical need among the higher levels of society. However, the trade did offer some measure of independence to the woman who wanted to make a good living by herself. The only alternative was the stage, and this was closely linked with prostitution in any case, as many actresses had to earn extra cash outside the theatre.

At the top of the tree, prostitutes lived in comfortable houses and apartments in districts such as Pimlico, St. John's Wood and Chelsea. Many in this class were kept by rich men and could afford to ride in fashionable costume in Hyde Park, which scandalised many Victorians. The district which became the 'focus of smart and competitive harlotry' lay between Regent Street and the Strand. Near here were the high-class brothels, found in places such as James Street, King's Place, Curzon Street and Oxenden Street. However, the inmates of these places were at a disadvantage to their sisters who could display their looks in the Haymarket area to potential clients. The area was described in *Household Words* as

. . . absolutely hideous at night with its sparring snobs,
and flashing satins, and sporting gents, and painted
cheeks . . .

When evening fell and the Haymarket theatres opened crowds
of heavily made-up prostitutes, including children, would
parade in the street, waiting for the theatregoers. The porticos
of the main theatres, and the near-by streets, were 'the most
celebrated whores' parades in the country' and high-class
prostitutes could be found in the saloons and passages of the
theatres themselves.

Beyond the Haymarket in Leicester Square and Regent Street,
in dark corners and night-houses, tastes according to pocket
could be satisfied. The whole area was in easy reach of Whitehall
and the London clubs, which supplied a regular and monied
clientele. Even the prostitutes who used the parks could earn
between three and six pounds a week. Each member of a colony
of French girls near Regent Street averaged twice as much. But
many rich men just visited the smart night-houses to find women.
Among the favourite houses of this type were Mott's, the Argyll
Rooms, Evan's and Kate Hamilton's. Mrs. Hamilton was a
well-known figure, fat and ugly, who presided over the saloon
from a high table. According to their income and status,
prostitutes could take clients back to nearby lodgings (Windmill
Street had several for the trade) or rent single rooms for short
periods. Many prostitutes preferred such arrangements because
they did not have to pay money to brothel owners or 'fancy
men'.

At the other end of the scale, were the sordid and squalid
environments where women similar to Jack the Ripper's victims
operated. These areas included Whitechapel, Waterloo Road,
Wapping and Ratcliffe Highway. The most infamous area for
prostitution was Bluegate Fields, which catered for sailors from
the Docks.

Bracebridge Hemyng, Mayhew's collaborator, described a
Bluegate prostitute he encountered. She was endeavouring to
get satisfaction from a pipe of opium.

Her face was grimy and unwashed, and her hands so
black and filthy that mustard-and-cress might have
been sown on them. As she was huddled up with her

back against the wall she appeared an animated bundle
of rags. She was apparently a powerfully mad woman,
and although her face was wrinkled and careworn, she
did not look exactly decrepit, but more like one
thoroughly broken down in spirit than in body. In all
probability she was diseased; and the disease com-
municated by the Malays, Lascars, and Orientals
generally, is said to be the most frightful form of lues
to be met in Europe. It goes by the name of the Dry—,
and is much dreaded by all the women in the neighbour-
hood of the docks.

Apart from the proximity of regular robbery and murder in
slum conditions, dockside prostitutes had to contend with
exuberant sailors who wanted to celebrate their liberty at the
end of a long voyage by spending all their money on a spree.
However, a clever 'Judy' could make sure that most of her
client's pay went through her hands.

In *London Labour and the London Poor*, John Binny described
some more dregs of the prostitute class:

. . . Some bloated, dissipated, and brutal in appear-
ance; others pale and wasted by want and suffering.
Many of them resort to bilking for a livelihood, that is,
they inveigle persons to low houses of bad fame, but do
not allow them to have criminal dealings with them.
Possibly the bodies of some may be covered with
dreadful disease, which they take care to conceal.
While in these houses they often indulge in the grossest
indecencies, too abominable to be mentioned, with old
grey-headed men on the very edge of the grave. Many
of these women are old convicted thieves of sixty years
of age and upwards. Strange to say, old men and boys
go with these withered crones, and sometimes fashion-
able gentlemen on a lark are to be seen walking arm
and arm with them, and even to enter their houses.

Binny was also interested in the class of prostitutes called
soldiers' women:

They are from sixteen to thirty years of age, and several

even older. Some have been in the streets for seventeen years and upwards. They live in the greatest poverty, covered with rags and filth, and many of them covered with horrid sores, and eruptions on their body, arms and legs, presenting in many cases a revolting appearance. Many of them have not the delicacy of females and live as pigs in a sty . . . In the middle of the day they sometimes wash their skirt, the only decent garment many of them have—their under clothing being a tissue of rags . . .

Two acts changed the appearances of prostitution. The first, the Criminal Law Amendment Act of 1885, effectively banned procuring and brothel-house keeping by imposing fines and imprisonment for these activities. The result was that prostitution went underground and many girls became 'self-employed'. The second was the Street Offences Act of 1959 which drove women off the streets effectively but not completely into other professions. Soho, Balham, Bayswater, and Notting Hill retained their interests. The car and the display card in newsagents'

The soldier cannot afford to employ professional women to gratify his passions, and if he were to do so, he must make the acquaintance of a very low set of women, who in all probability will communicate some infectious disease to him. He feels he is never safe, and he is only too glad to seize the opportunity of forming an intimacy with a woman who will appreciate him for his own sake, cost him nothing but the trouble of taking her about occasionally, and who, whatever else she may do, will never by any chance infect. I heard that some of the privates in the Blues and the brigade of Guards often formed very reprehensible connections with women of property, tradesmen's wives, and even ladies, who supplied them with money, and behaved with the greatest generosity to them, only stipulating for the preservation of secrecy in their intrigues.

Bracebridge Hemyng writing on Prostitution in London in *London Labour and the London Poor*, 1861.

shops became the new media of communication:

Qualified lady offers comprehensive French lessons.

The year 1959 was also the time when Attilio Messina was imprisoned for four years and afterwards deported. Attilio was one of the five notorious Messina brothers who were known as the Vice Kings of Mayfair and who had turned prostitution into big-time business. Salvatore, Alfredo, Eugenio, Attilio and Carmelo were the sons of a Sicilian who had set up a string of brothels around the Mediterranean. In 1934, Eugenio came to London to extend the family's operations and within ten years was earning one thousand pounds a week from a string of continental girls. Eugenio sent for his family to help him run this gold-mine of a business. Soon the five brothers had acquired flats and houses in fashionable districts of London in which they installed their girls.

In contrast to the girls of Boswell's time who made casual, friendly encounters where they could, the Messina prostitutes were subjected to a rigid discipline. A typical Messina girl was forbidden to go outside her own small beat or to take up any other job. She was not allowed to waste time either by talking with friends and colleagues or by allowing clients to spend more than ten minutes with her. She had to hand over all the money she earned, which was usually collected daily. To keep an eye on her and maintain an even 'work-flow', she had a maid, an ex-prostitute no longer an attractive proposition to men. Every Messina girl, of course, had to be discreet and she was encouraged to work hard by the threat of violence.

For a long time, the police could not prove that the Messina vice empire existed. Fines for soliciting were paid promptly in cash and the girl concerned would immediately return to her beat.

The Second World War brought some setbacks to the Messinas. They were forced to use British girls because foreign girls were no longer available to meet the demands of the public. The brothers themselves had to take steps to avoid military service. Still, however, they had twenty girls in 1947 earning some fifty to one hundred pounds per night. They had also hired a 'sergeant-major'—an ex-prostitute from France—to supervise and train younger recruits. In the same year, the

Messinas tangled with a Maltese gang who had demanded protection from some of their prostitutes. While the Maltese were imprisoned for demanding money with menaces, Eugenio was also jailed for three years, for wounding one of the gang and Carmelo went to prison, too, for attempting to bribe a Wandsworth prison officer to show favour to Eugenio. While the brothers were inside, their girls continued to deposit their earnings with the other Messinas.

In 1950, *The People* newspaper exposed the Messinas. As a result, all the brothers except Alfredo fled to the Continent. However, the police were able to arrest Alfredo later for bribery and living on immoral earnings and subsequently he was imprisoned for two years. For a time, the Messina ring continued to operate, even with the brothers not on the scene. They attempted to start a similar operation in Belgium but the Belgian police arrested Carmelo and Eugenio in 1955. Eugenio was imprisoned for seven years but Carmelo was able to return to Britain. Carmelo eventually died in Italy after being imprisoned, then deported from Britain. Attilio and Eugenio were eventually deported to Italy, too. Alfredo, who continued to live in Britain, died in 1963 and Salvatore went to Switzerland.

When Attilio Messina was tried at the Old Bailey in 1959 for procuring a dressmaker and living on her immoral earnings, it was disclosed that she had made forty thousand pounds for the Messinas during the ten years she had worked for them.

The Recorder, Sir Gerald Dodson, told Attilio:

> *You made a sumptuous but revolting living from the suffering bodies of the women you trapped, seduced and reduced to a form of slavery. You caused great suffering and it is only right and just that you should also suffer.*

Considering the loyalty of many of the Messina girls to the brothers, their 'suffering' may have been less than appeared. But never since has prostitution in London been exploited on so large a scale. The oldest profession has now returned to its original method of getting business—a smile and a friendly invitation from a doorway.

CHAPTER THIRTEEN

PILLORY AND PORN

In the year 1560 a maid was set upon the Pillory for giving her mistress and her household poison. Besides the shame of the Pillory, one of her ears were cut, and she was burnt on the Brow. And two days after she was set again on the Pillory, and her other ear cut. And but some days after, another maid was set on the Pillory for the same crime; and her ear cut, and burnt on the brow.

THUS JOHN STOW'S *A Survey of London* describes the fate of two victims sentenced to a spell in the pillory. Women were often sentenced to this fate for offences such as child-beating, procuring and prostitution. Pillories were used for two purposes; they exposed their prisoners, male and female, to public humiliation, and they enabled the public, if it so wished, to inflict injury on the culprits. The sentence of being held by neck and hands in a huge immovable collar was usually augmented by some other punishment such as flogging or, as we have seen, branding and mutilation.

In London, well-known pillories were situated at Cheapside, West Smithfield, Westminster, Charing Cross and Seven Dials. A short period in any one could be fatal. In 1751, two highwaymen, Egan and Salmon, were sentenced to stand in the West Smithfield pillory prior to their imprisonment. A vindictive mob (for the two criminals had committed robbery and murder) gathered round and pelted them with missiles. In less than half an hour, Egan was struck dead by a stone, and Salmon was injured so badly that he died later. The same fate befell the robber and perjurer John Waller, who died after being pelted in the pillory at Seven Dials in 1732.

If you wrote, published or printed literature which offended authority on political or obscene grounds, you were liable to be pilloried or have your books burnt, or worse, depending on whom you offended. Stow related how one William Carter, a printer, a man who had been imprisoned several times for printing seditious books, went too far in 1584. He was hanged, drawn and quartered at Tyburn for printing the seditious book *A Treatise in Schisme*. A noteworthy burning was ordered by the Archbishop of Canterbury in the Hall of the Company of Stationers in 1599, when eleven books, four of them 'lewd', were burnt. But John Lilburn in 1637 for printing and publishing seditious literature, was sentenced in the Star Chamber to be whipped through the streets of Westminster and confined on the pillory. Daniel Defoe was pilloried, too, in 1703 for writing *The Shortest Way with the Dissenters*, a satirical work which infuriated the High Church Tories.

During the Restoration period, the government were particularly sensitive to literature which might ridicule them. The result was the Licensing Act of 1662 by which every printed book required a government licence. The Act lapsed in 1695, but until 1697, government officials such as the Inspector of Printing Presses were given a warrant to

> . . . *Search in all printing houses and elsewhere and to apprehend such authors, printers, bookbinders, hawkers, newswriters and others as shall be found to distribute unlicenced false and scandalous books, prints, manuscripts, papers etc.*

Even after that, writers and publishers were in danger of government action from time to time. In 1725 the famous bookseller Edmund Curll was arrested for obscenity for publishing *The Nun in her Smock* and *The Treatise of Flogging*. After some months in the King's Bench Prison, Curll stood in the pillory at Charing Cross. The attendant crowd thought it a great joke, and, when Curll was released, bore him off to the nearest tavern. Curll was one of the publishers and writers who belonged to the period of literary output known as Grub Street. The best-known writers of this school were Tom Brown and Ned Ward. Grub Street literature has been described as 'lively, racy, at times salacious and deliberately shocking, but most always interesting'.*

In Victorian times, the obscene publication trade was centred on Holywell Street. Henry Mayhew investigated:

> *The penny song-books (which are partly indecent), and entitled the 'Sam Hall' and 'Ross' Songsters are seldom or never sold in the streets. Many of those vended in the shops outrage all decency. Some of these are styled the 'Coal-Hole Companion', 'Cider-Cellar Songs', 'Captain Morris's Songs', &c. (the filthiest of all). These are generally marked 1s. and sold at 6d.; and have a coloured frontispiece. They are published chiefly by H. Smith, Holywell Street . . . Some titles are unprintable.*

Mayhew also came across the 'sham indecent trade', in which hawkers would sell packets wrapped in coloured paper, leading their victims to believe that the packets contained improper or scandalous publications. The packet, of course, never contained anything indecent.

Bracebridge Hemyng, contributor to *London Labour and the London Poor*, remarked:

> *There are book-hawkers, who go about the country, having first filled their wallets from the filthy cellars of Holywell Street, sowing the seeds of immorality; ser-vants in country houses will pay, without hesitation large prices for improper books.*

Hemyng mentions 'a man called Dugdale, who has gone grey in this disgusting occupation', and who was brought before a magistrate for selling obscene prints, and also sending some to customers in the country.

> *He had been engaged in this infamous and diabolical*

---

* **Philip Pinkus**, *Grub Street Stripped Bare* **(Constable).**

traffic nearly forty years, and had spent a great number
of them in prison at various times; tons weight of
obscene books, pictures, and plates had been seized
upon his premises.

Since then, society has become more tolerant of the written
word in publications which a century ago would have been
regarded as obscene. One watershed in the change of taste was
the trial in 1954 of the publishers Secker & Warburg and others
for obscene libel. Secker & Warburg had published the American
novel *The Philanderer* by Stanley Kauffman, and the test of
obscenity was that extracted from a decision of 1868, i.e.,
'whether the tendency of the matter charged as obscene was
to deprave and corrupt those whose minds are open to such
immoral influences and into whose hands such a publication
may fall'. Mr. Justice Stable in his summing up at the Central
Criminal Court said:

> *The literature of the world from the earliest times,*
> *when people first learned to write—literature sacred*
> *and profane, poetry and prose—represents the sum*
> *total of human thought throughout the ages and from*
> *all the varied civilisations the human pilgrimage has*
> *traversed. Are we going to say in England that our*
> *contemporary literature is to be measured by what is*
> *suitable for the fourteen-year-old schoolgirl to read?*

The jury thought No, and returned verdicts of Not Guilty in
respect of all accused.

The Philanderer was followed into court at intervals by famous
titles such as *Lady Chatterly's Lover* and *Fanny Hill*. But the
dam had broken. From now on, serious literature published in
London could be franker about basic human functions. Less
highbrow literature, particularly that which was visual as
opposed to written, could be even franker. The permissive
society, salacious court cases and the sex-shop trend of the
Scandinavians encouraged the speedy growth of relevant business enterprises such as pornographic bookshops. Eric Clark in
Len Deighton's *London Dossier* (Penguin 1967) describes what
could be found behind the scenes in a typical Soho porn shop
during the late sixties:

The room inside will certainly be tiny, with books grouped along two or three of the walls, divided into two main sections, straight 'porn' and sadism. A fair price for unillustrated books (sample titles Keep It In The Family *and* The Sexual Life Of Robinson Crusoe) *would be £3–£5 and for illustrated material between £6 and £9. Photographs, usually in sets of five, are filed. Inquirers, you will note, are specific: women duos, lesbians, groups. Price: not more than £1 a set.*

By the seventies, London had acquired a sound reputation for being a centre for the making and distribution of pornography, especially blue films. Said a Soho distributor:

We call them 'reelers' in the trade. They come in 8mm and 16mm, black-and-white and colour, and in 16mm with sound, too. A colour and sound movie will cost about £30 in the trade, but you could get an 8mm version for around £5 wholesale.

Costs of making blue films were cheaper in London than in Denmark, so a thriving export smuggling business built up with products going to Scandinavia and Germany. In 1970, British customs officials seized 1,500,000 books and films, and one estimate of the trade was £50 million a year.

It was the scope of this trade, plus the prosecution of the publishers of *Oz* magazine, that persuaded Lord Longford to make his unique private report on pornography in 1972. While the market expanded rapidly during a decade, history has demonstrated that the pendulum of taste swings backwards and forwards from century to century. With no sign forthcoming to indicate a changing trend and a decline in the demands for pornography, porn pedlars were 'selling lays while the sun shone'.

For them, there was no equivalent of the pillory.

CHAPTER FOURTEEN

BODIES AND BURIALS

To church, and with the grave-maker, chose a place for my brother to lie in, just under my mother's pew. But to see how a man's tomb are at the mercy of such a fellow, that for sixpence he would (as his own words were): 'I will jostle them together but I will make room for him', speaking of the fullness of the middle aisle, where he was to lie, and that he would for my father's sake do my brother that is dead, all the civility he can; which was to disturb others' corps that are not quite rotten, to make room for him.

It was in March 1664 that Pepys went along to the church of St. Bride, Fleet Street, to make arrangements for the burial of his brother Tom. Here he came across one of London's major problems, the overcrowding of churches and churchyards where the burial of the dead was concerned.

Back in the twelfth century, according to William Fitzstephen, London had 126 churches, most of which were within the walls of the city. London's dead were thus buried in the precincts of these churches, either in the building or in the churchyard. The crowding of the dead came about with the rise in population and the change of London into an entirely commercial city. While churches within the walls were being closed down, there were not enough outside the walls in residential quarters to hold the dead comfortably.

If there were many dead people to bury all at once, open spaces were commandeered. For example, 50,000 plague victims were buried at Smithfield at the time of the Black Death, as were 1,100 Quakers in a pit at Bunhill Fields during the plague of 1665. Pepys was 'much troubled' to hear that plague victims were being buried in the open Tothill Fields at Westminster. Tothill Fields was also used for the burying place of about 1,200 Scots soldiers captured at the Battle of Worcester in 1651, according to the parish records of St. John the Evangelist, Westminster.

But as far as the churches went, they were virtually the only places for the normal disposal of the dead and their tiny church-yards presented nauseous sights and smells, with burials piled on burials and crammed charnel houses. Much of this was hidden from mourners, because funerals usually took place at night, with church bells tolling in the dark. This nocturnal custom took place until at least the early nineteenth century, and probably stemmed from the ancient belief that the shadow 'as a non-material extension of the person, was in fact the soul'. Spirits as such were not welcome at funerals. In the eighteenth century, the most popular time for burials was eight or nine in the evening. In the old ballad of Cock Robin:

> Who'll be the clerk?
> I, said the Lark,
> If it's not in the dark,
> I'll be the clerk.

> Who'll carry the link?
> I, said the Linnet,
> I'll fetch it in a minute,
> I'll carry the link.

> Who'll carry the coffin?
> I, said the Kite,
> If it's not through the night,
> I'll carry the coffin.

Since the Burial Laws Amendment Act of 1880, burials must take place during the hours of daylight. People had to be buried by day during the 1665 plague, as Pepys notes:

> *The people die so, that now it seems they are fain*

*to carry the dead to be buried by day-light, the nights
not sufficing to do it in.*

He was very concerned with infection from plague victims.

*. . . but Lord! to consider the madness of the people
of the town, who will (because they are forbid) come
in crowds along with the dead corpses to see them
buried.*

The inadequacies of London's graveyards became particularly
and gruesomely apparent during the plague. The sheer numbers
of deaths at the plague's peak (sometimes 1,000 a day) over-
whelmed the capacity of London's tiny churchyards. Bodies,
which should have been buried six feet deep, were hastily laid,
crowded together, just below the surface. Later, when all available wood had run out, corpses were uncoffined. The result
was an overpowering, nauseous stench that prevailed even in
cold weather, making the occupation of houses near churchyards impossible. The appalling stench remained over the
churchyards until the bodies rotted away.

When the churchyards had reached their limit for burials,
parishes took action by digging huge holes known as plague
pits in open spaces. Daniel Defoe in *A Journal of the Plague
Year* describes them:

*Into these pits they had put perhaps fifty or sixty
bodies each; then they made larger holes, wherein they
buried all that the cart brought in a week, which, by
the middle to the end of August, came to from 200 to
400 a week; and they could not dig them larger, because
of the order of the magistrates confining them to leave
no bodies within six feet of the surface . . .*

It was to these huge graves that the melancholy convoys of
dead carts made their way with loads of blackened, putrefying
corpses. Even the plague pits were inadequate at one time and
bodies had to be piled in the streets until the over-worked
gravediggers had prepared the next pit. The dead carts and their
crews for many sufferers had more links with the underworld
than with real life. Every night the carts trundled around the

parishes preceded by men bearing flickering torches and announced to each street by bellmen with heavy handbells. The chilling call of the drivers and bearers became the historical motto of the plague: 'Bring out your dead! Bring out your dead!'

The bearers and drivers were easily recruited from the large numbers of unemployed found in London at this time. Many of the dead cart crews were former servants to rich families who, on leaving the infected city for their country houses, tended to dismiss their entire staffs. Dead cart men had to be rough and insensitive; their clothing stank of vomit and faeces and more often than not they were reeling drunk as they pulled festering bodies out of houses and slung them into the carts. The alleys and narrow passageways near Coleman Street presented horrific problems. The dead carts were too large to penetrate the warren and the dead had to be man-handled through the small openings to the waiting convoys. The grave-diggers, who never rested, also had their problems. One is described by James Leasor in *The Plague and The Fire*:

> *Near Aldgate churchyard the parish authorities sunk a pit fifty feet long, twenty feet across and about ten feet deep. The first body was tipped into this on September 6th, and soon it was full of corpses, either naked or at best wrapped in old shirts or strips of blanket. Day after day, as more cadavers were shovelled in from the dead-carts at one end, labourers hacked away earth and stones at the other to enlarge the pit. Finally they could extend it no more; a wall was in the way. So they began to dig down. They reached a depth of twenty feet before they came to water, which bubbled in among the rotting corpses.*

When the plague was over, Pepys was still concerned with the situation.

> *This is the first time I have been in the church since I left London for the plague, and it frighted me indeed to go through the church more than I thought it could have done, to see so many graves lie so high upon the*

churchyards where people had been buried of the plague.
I was much troubled at it, and do not think to go
through it again a good while. I find many about the
City that live near the churchyards solicitous to have
the churchyards covered with lime, and I think it is
needfull, and ours I hope will be done.

But not all corpses 'frighted' Pepys, as he records on seeing the
body of Henry V's wife in Westminster Abbey, 1669:

> *. . . there did see all the tombs very finely, having one*
> *with us alone and here-we did see, by particular favour,*
> *the body of Queen Katherine of Valois; and I had the*
> *upper part of her body in my hands, and I did kiss her*
> *mouth, reflecting upon it that I did kiss a queen, and*
> *that this was my birth-day, thirty-six years old, that I*
> *did kiss a queene.*

The lady now lies under a modern altar covered with an ancient
slab in the Chantry Chapel. She died in 1437.

Pepys returned to the Abbey for the funeral three years later
of Admiral Lord Sandwich, killed in action during a naval
action against the Dutch. The dead Admiral was borne by
barge from Deptford to Westminster, mourned by 'the King,
the Duke of York, and all the principal nobles and officers of
England'. The most comparable occasion in modern times must
have been the funeral of Sir Winston Churchill, whose body was
conveyed up the river from the Tower of London to Waterloo
in 1965.

~~~~~~

> Rossetti in a gesture brave
> Laid his verse in Lizzie's grave.
> Seven years passed by, and then
> He went and dug them up again.

In October, 1869, by the light of a midnight fire, friends of
Dante Gabriel Rossetti raised the coffin of his wife Elizabeth
from the family grave at Highgate Cemetery, opened it, and
removed the manuscript book of poems he had buried with her.

~~~~~~

Death in eighteenth-century London was an expensive procedure for the family of the deceased. You would receive formal notification of a death from a black-edged card covered with symbols such as skulls and wreaths. If you visited the house of mourning (it was, of course, curtained and shuttered), you would probably see a professional mourner outside hired by the bereaved to display signs of grief and desolation. Inside the house, you would be handed black gloves with which to hold the mugs of beer and wine that went with the mourning feast. The body would be on view, with features made up, in the coffin. You paid your respects to the deceased in a room hung with black cloth and lit with tall candles which surrounded the coffin.

Undertakers at this time operated very elegant establishments, displaying coffins 'of every kind and colour' and funerary ornaments of wide variety. Many undertakers lit their shops at night 'like our own jewellers and dress shops', giving a macabre effect to the dimly lit streets of the time. Apart from the expenses of the undertaker, there were high fees for the digging of a grave in a churchyard. For instance, the cost of burying a three-year-old child, 'a child of one of the lower sort of people', in a churchyard was two guineas.

When the condition of most London churchyards in this century is considered, it is not surprising that expenses were high. Bernard Ash describes it in *The Golden City*:

> . . . *the greater part of the mortal remains of the ordinary members of City parishes were stuffed by hook or by crook into the microscopic churchyards of the churches where they had worshipped. The ground had already been used for burials time and time over and was no longer made up of soil but of bone, rotten wood and human decay. The practice was in theory that coffins and their contents should be allowed to rot until there was nothing left but bone: the bones were then disinterred and piled in a charnel house, while what was left of the decayed wood was burned. In fact the demands for space were such that nothing like the necessary time could be allowed for complete decay . . .*

Francis Bancroft, a city official who died in 1727, had an

original idea about the disposal of his body. Having left a large sum of money to the Draper's Company, he instructed that his body should be embalmed and placed in a square tomb with a hinged lid (built in his lifetime) erected in the church of St. Helen, Bishopsgate. This was to enable his body to be inspected at intervals. Officers of the Drapers' Company carried out this duty for over 100 years but the inspection became so distasteful that it was concluded.

At the end of the century the graveyards in which the poor of London were buried were an appalling source of stench. The technique was to dig a huge grave capable of holding seven tiers of coffins with four or so coffins to each tier. The pit was not covered over before it was filled and so the smell of decaying bodies hung over it. The same happened with similar communal graves dug in other graveyards.

Malodorous or not, it seems that many courting couples in this period, especially from the lower orders, found that some graveyards were ideal for evening meetings. Presumably, the most favourite churchyards were those with less pressure on them for space and therefore they must have been on the edges of London, if not in surrounding villages.

At this time, it was still customary to bury suicides at cross-roads in the parish where they killed themselves. Also, each body would have a stake driven through it. This, for instance, happened to a condemned prisoner in Newgate in 1793 when he committed suicide. His body, clothed and fettered with the face covered with a white cloth, was laid on a plank and driven on an open cart to the top of Holborn Hill. There, it was laid in a deep pit opposite the end of Hatton Garden with a stake hammered through the chest. The custom ended in 1823 when a suicide was buried immediately opposite the grounds of

---

The body of Dr. John Hunter, the famous surgeon who died in 1793, is buried in the nave of Westminster Abbey. It was first laid to rest in the crypt of St. Martin-in-the-Fields. In 1859, Frank Buckland, the naturalist, searched for Hunter's coffin among 2,266 others and found it after sixteen days. Hunter's coffin was the 2,264th that Buckland examined.

Buckingham Palace where Hobart Place meets Grosvenor Gardens. George IV objected strongly and within a month, an Act of Parliament had abolished the custom.

One of the most well-known burial grounds in London was Bunhill Fields, for two centuries the chief burying place of Nonconformists. The notice outside the entrance gate claims that more than 120,000 bodies were buried there. In the sixteenth century, bones from the charnel chapel of old St. Paul's Cathedral were deposited there, from which the name Bonehill and then Bunhill is derived. From 1665, the year of the plague, Bunhill Fields was in use as a graveyard. In 1716, the Quaker section was vulnerable to body snatchers and so all gates but one were ordered to be closed at dusk. In 1852, an Order in Council forbade further burials in Bunhill Fields and an Act of Parliament in 1867 prevented the secular use of the area for purposes such as building. From then on, the city corporation has been responsible for its upkeep and preservation as an open space. Among people buried at Bunhill Fields were John Bunyan; Daniel Defoe; Isaac Watts, the hymn-writer; Susannah Wesley, mother of John and Charles Wesley; William Blake; Robert Tilling, executed at Tyburn in 1760 for murdering his master; and Henry Fauntleroy the banker, hanged at Newgate in 1824 for forgery.

In the church of St. James Garlickhithe, when the vaults were being finally closed in 1839, a body in almost complete preservation was found. Choir-boys at the church used to take the skeleton for 'a run round'. It is now kept in a cupboard.

By mid-nineteenth century, London's water supply, sewers and burial grounds were at their most insanitary. In 1849, the cholera outbreak at its height killed four hundred people a day. There were now 218 acres of shallow and packed graveyards, described as 'grotesque, noisome, gruesome'. Those at St. Andrew's, Holborn, and St. Bride's (where Tom Pepys was buried) were especially horrific. At last, authority acted. In 1852 an Act concerning the Burial of the Dead in the Metropolis stopped burials in City churchyards, but each churchyard, as in the case of Bunhill Fields, had to have an individual Order in Council. This enabled churches such as St. Mary-le-Bow, Cheapside, to continue to bury bodies in the crypt until 1860. The new city cemetery was established at Ilford. Before the act, a committee of the House of Commons heard that sixty loads of 'loam of human remains' from a burial ground in St. Clement's Lane were used in the make-up of Waterloo Road. The churchyard at St. Margaret's, Westminster was a 'nuisance' at this time, and after a report in 1850, a new burial ground was procured off the Fulham Road. The combination of the evil-smelling Thames on one side and the St. Margaret's churchyard on the other must have made the Houses of Parliament almost intolerable to visit during summer months.

Earlier reform of London's graveyards had been opposed by parish officials who not only resented government interference in local matters but also wished to preserve financial interests. For instance, several parishes contained family tombs on which dues were paid. The destruction of such tombs in the interests of reform and sanitation would end a regular source of revenue.

In the meantime, fashionable cemeteries had been opening in the suburbs. All contained a wide assortment of tombs, obelisks and urns in classical and Gothic style. Kensal Green was opened in 1832. It is a cemetery of about 70 acres and contains some 50,000 graves. Several well-known writers and artists were buried here, including Thackeray, W. Harrison Ainsworth, Leigh Hunt, Wilkie Collins, Anthony Trollope, John Leech, James Ward and William Mulready. The distinguished engineers Brunel, father and son, and the operatic singer Madame Vestris have their graves here, too. In 1872, a coffin bearer was killed at Kensal Green when a lead coffin was accidently dropped on him.

A contemporary cemetery of the time is the Brompton (West London and Westminster) Cemetery, opened in 1840. Buried here are two sporting figures; Robert Coombes, the champion sculler, and John 'Gentleman' Jackson, the prize-fighter. Coombes's tomb has the inscription 'Oars, coat and badge, farewell', supporting watermen at each corner and above an overturned skiff in stone. Jackson's tomb is carved with the figures of athletes.

Privileged visitors can visit the Bromptom 'catacombs', underground vaults with tiers of coffins placed there in the last century. The wooden outer covers are rotting, exposing the lead linings. Some of the dead in the vaults fought at Waterloo.

A cemetery which has been described as strange, romantic and poignant is Highgate Cemetery which contains about 45,000 graves. Among those buried here are Michael Faraday, George

Eliot, Karl Marx and Christina Rossetti. The cemetery has many examples of curious sepulchral art such as the tomb of Frederick William Lillywhite which has a wicket struck by a ball to indicate that he was out for the last time. The tomb of George Wombwell, the famous menagerie man, has a sleeping lion and that of Tom Sayers, the prize-fighter, shows himself and his dog.

Between 1880 and 1915, three hundred pets—mostly dogs— were buried in the Dogs' Cemetery at the Victoria Gate, Hyde Park. The exceptions are a few cats and birds. The cemetery began when the Duke of Cambridge, when ranger of the park, obtained permission for his wife to bury her dog there. Each pet had its own tombstone, but several graves hold more than one animal from the same household which was necessary when all the available ground in the cemetery was used up.

The coming of cremation eased the pressures on space for burying the dead. The first move came from the Queen's surgeon Sir Henry Thompson, who had been impressed with cremation methods carried out on the Continent. In 1874, Sir Henry published *Cremation: the Treatment of the Body after Death*, written with the sordid conditions of many cemeteries in mind. In the same year, the Cremation Society of Great Britain was founded. But progress was slow, with church and government against the principle. The breakthrough came in 1884 after Dr. William Price attempted to cremate his child in South Wales. The subsequent legal action produced the judgement that cremation was a legal process, provided that it did not create a nuisance. But eighteen years passed before the Cremation Act became law. This Act regulated cremation and called for a special series of death certificates to prevent any evidence of murder being destroyed for ever.

At the end of the Victorian age, then, the disposal of dead bodies in London finally became unobtrusive to sight and sense. It was one, as we have seen, of several municipal amenities to undergo reform in order to cope with the vast increase of population. As with many other kinds of social reform, 'things got worse before they got better', or, as in many cases, healthier. There was a vicious roundabout of linked circumstances joined by more and more people and only changing attitudes could and did halt it. In simplification, the roundabout was made up something like this:

More people
  meant
More sewage
  meant
Inadequate sewers
  meant
More disease
  meant
More deaths
  meant
Inadequate graveyards
  meant
More disease
  meant
More deaths
  meant
Larger families
  meant
More people etc

The reform of the disposal of dead bodies also meant that no longer did Londoners have to live with reminders of death all around them. Death, like the other functions of life, had won some privacy at last.

CHAPTER FIFTEEN

CHANGE FOR THE BETTER

London is a modern Babylon.
(Tancred, *Book 5, Chapter 5*)

THE FIGURATIVE meaning of Babylon is rich and dissolute. Certainly London, represented by large financial institutions in the city, can be called rich, and London exemplified by West End night-life could be described as dissolute at times. You might even talk of a Tower of Babel, if you consider the large number of visitors from abroad who come to London. But these qualities apart, has London's reputation today really improved? Londoners still fight and murder each other. Immigrants still cause problems as they did in mediaeval times. Vagrants still sleep outside in dark corners. Crowded living, packed streets, noise—the heart of London still has the same characteristics as of old. And streaks of evil still show at intervals. In the 1960's, the art of Rachmanism meant intimidating tenants to pay high rents. Every now and then, a major financial fraud is exposed. At times, shattering violence breaks out in quiet streets when banks are raided. Many public buildings such as prisons and hospitals can show conditions which belong to another age. Babylon or beautiful city; some sides to London will never change.

But change there has been, and most of it during the latter half of the nineteenth century. We have seen how the role of the city changed from a town centre to the axis of a commercial empire and in doing so relinquished its responsibility to its poor classes. Why? Because the poor were not needed any more to sustain its life. What was needed was a skilled literate class to keep the machinery of commerce moving and this was readily forthcoming in a society that created many class levels. The great yardstick was wealth, and wealth was flooding in to city firms and managers as British investment overseas sucked in its profits. However, the London poor were not as badly off as their contemporaries in the provinces who through the industrial revolution and the enclosing of land, were living in atrocious slums and working in depressing factories. The poor began to realise that they must help themselves and so the first moves towards trade unionism were made.

Industrial advance in London helped to shift the poor even farther away. The new railways and later, new underground lines and buses, made it easier for the army of clerks to travel to work from the suburbs. At the same time, stations, track and modern roads were built where some of the worst slums had existed, so that the poor (and many of the lowest dregs of society) had to move. The building of Victoria Street demolished many of the hideous slums of Westminster. Shaftesbury Avenue helped to open up the rookery of Seven Dials. Necessity and reform together constructed new sewers, bridges and grave-yards. Brighter street lighting was extended, and while many of the building schemes initiated had a bleak uniformity, London was now able to see and breathe to a greater extent. Just as important, it could also cope with its still-expanding population.

It was becoming fashionable to be respectable, and behind this trend were the preachings of the evangelical movement whose doctrines helped to keep many of the working classes from revolution. Their main message was: be content with your lot on earth however bad it is, because you'll get a just reward in the next life. However, the social conscience of the rich was stirring. Writers such as Dickens were describing the abysmal lives of the London poor, and public curiosity helped to bring about needed changes. One significant change, indeed an advance, was the Education Act of 1870 which introduced com-pulsory schooling. This act was not only a means to help the working class improve themselves and eventually their social environment but also it was a safety valve against the more militant demands of trade unionism.

Attitudes towards criminal punishment were softening, too. One of the first acts in Victoria's reign abolished the pillory. Another act cut the number of capital offences. There were still public executions outside Newgate and other prisons for the next thirty years, but society now had less demand for vicious deterrents. For one thing, the concept of long prison sentences was gaining popularity and for the other, London's professional police force came into being in 1829. Crime prevention was now as important as detection and punishment.

The new Metropolitan Police Force joined the successful Bow Street Runners and Horse Patrol and consisted of two thousand constables in blue frockcoats. The conspicuousness of the coats and the fact that the police were forbidden to enter public houses while on duty hampered the efficiency of the force at their birth. But by 1867 their numbers had risen to eight thousand and they were accepted fully by the public as protectors of law and order. A large part of London's evil character was now under control for good. The police proved their worth in the last half of the nineteenth century when London as well as Europe contained numbers of restless revolutionaries such as Fenians, Anarchists and Nihilists.

By the end of the century, standards of living had risen and the great mass of working people were now starting to enjoy 'some degree of modest comfort'. Wages had risen, prices had fallen and food was plentiful. Social life was improving with new sports and amusement to sample. As a result of being let out of what amounted to a cage of social repression, Londoners experienced general contentment with their new environment. Two world wars united all classes at the time with the result that former barriers between them became less rigid. The Welfare State was the final stage of a century of social reform. London was not so much evil now as amoral, as social attitudes became more and more liberal. Hence Babylon, if you like.

If you reverse the word 'evil', you get 'live'. With all the social, economic and technical changes which have happened to London from Victorian days, the vice-versa juxtaposition could be apt. Evil London has become Live London.